BUILDING PROCUREMENT SYSTEMS

(Second Edition)

BUILDING PROCUREMENT SYSTEMS

— a guide to building project management

(Second Edition)

by James Franks, FRICS, FCIOB, ACIArb

with additional material provided by
Peter Harlow, CEng, MIM, MIInfSci

The Chartered Institute of Building
Englemere, Kings Ride, Ascot, Berks, SL5 8BJ

British Library Cataloguing in Publication Data
Franks, James, *1927–*
    Building procurement systems.
    1. Construction industries. Project management
    I. Title II. Chartered Institute of Building
    624.0684

    ISBN 1-85380-014-7

    1st edition 1984
    2nd edition 1990
    Reprinted 1992

Printed and bound in Great Britain by J. W. Arrowsmith Ltd., Bristol

FOREWORD TO THE SECOND EDITION

The 1984 edition of *Building Procurement Systems* aimed to provide a simple guide to the various options available to building industry clients and their advisers. It has achieved a worldwide audience and been used as 'course notes' for numerous professional and academic courses. Peter Harlow's *Building Management Abstracts* have provided countless students with material for research.

This new edition builds on these foundations and incorporates developments which have occurred since 1983 when much of the earlier text was written. Peter Harlow has brought up-to-date his bibliography and revised the glossary.

New sections are included. The preface explains the purpose and principal features of the text.

James Franks
Department of Construction Management
South Bank Polytechnic
London BN7 2AD

July 1990

FOREWORD TO THE FIRST EDITION

In the years 1982–83 I wrote a series of articles dealing with non-traditional forms of contractual arrangement for *Building Trades Journal*. Subsequently, they were coordinated into a background paper for a seminar held at the Polytechnic of the South Bank in February, 1984, which attempted to provide a guide to the various systems available primarily for building industry clients.

Meanwhile, at the offices of The Chartered Institute of Building, Peter Harlow, Head of Information, was compiling information to complement the definitive work which would stem the flow of enquiry and establish some order from the minefield of definition and interpretation.

It was at his suggestion that this publication was produced, amplifying my original – but amended – text with a glossary of terms and a comprehensive bibliography.

The guide attempts to meet the needs of the client, the builder, the consultant, and students of all disciplines.

It is in four parts. The first section gives an introduction to the procurement systems in more-or-less common use. This is followed by a comparison of these systems from the standpoint of fitness for function, economy, speed and aesthetics.

The final two sections are a glossary of terms and a bibliography, the latter using material from that invaluable reference tool, *Building Management Abstracts*. These will hopefully, clarify the situation for those foundering in a sea of 'managements' and provide a resource for detailed studies.

James Franks
Lewes, 1984

ACKNOWLEDGEMENTS

Many thanks to the people who have helped to produce the 1990 edition.

In particular to Peter Harlow who, as before, has contributed the bibliography with abstracts and the glossary, which are major parts of the text. He has been a constant help.

To colleagues at South Bank Polytechnic who have helped with contributions, proof reading and correction and in other ways.

To Julian Vickery at Greycoat, sometime student at South Bank, whose contribution is mentioned in the text.

To Ron Denny, former deputy director, British Property Federation, John Newton, Christopher Hogg and Ross Shute at Bovis, Jeff Wild at Costain Project Management, Graham Love at Jones Lang Wootton and David Wheater at Balfour Beatty who provided facts regarding the activities of their respective organisations.

To Nigel Bentley and to the 50 firms, listed below, who provided information for the survey which provided the material for Section 6 and to Simon Ralf of Peat Marwick McClintock with whom findings of mutual interest were exchanged.

To the editors of *Architects Journal, Building, Building Design, Building Today, Chartered Builder, Chartered Quantity Surveyor, Chartered Surveyors Weekly, Contract Journal* and *Estates Gazette* who kindly published an open letter which provided many points of contact with people with similar interests and concerns whose contributions have influenced the text.

Clients who contributed to survey

Arnold Project Services for Kumagi Gumi
B & Q
Barclays Bank
Basildon District Council
BP Oil UK
Brentwood Roman Catholic Diocese
British Airways Property Development Department
British Rail
Church View Surgery
Citycorp Investment
Cloth Kits
Cornwall County Council
County and District Properties
Crest Estates

Dartford Borough Council
Darlington Health Authority
Fitzwilliam College, Cambridge
Fleetway House Construction Management
Gatwick Airport
Grenada Studio Tours
Greycoat Group
Grosvenor Developments
Harrison Homes
Imry Merchants
Land Securities
London Docklands Development Corporation
Luton Football Club
Lysander Group
National Gallery Services
Norfolk Capital Hotels
Nuffield Hospitals
Plessey Property
Printers Charitable Corporation
Property Services Agency
Retirement Security
River Lodge Surgery
Sainsbury's Homebase
Saint Martin's Property
Saint Pancras Housing Association
South West Thames Health
Standard Chartered Bank
Sussex Housing Association for the Aged
Westminster Roman Catholic Diocesan Trustees
Willis Faber
Wimpey International
Windsor, Royal Borough of
To others who advised or assisted but whose names have been inadvertently mislaid, my thanks and apologies for my omission.

James Franks
January 1990

CONTENTS

Contents

GLOSSARY

COLLABORATION CONTRACT

A variant of the negotiated approach where, having established a price for the project, the client and contractor agree a sum to be included in the builder's price for the management of the construction phase. Part of this to be paid to the client in return for secondment of a senior member of the client's organisation to act as construction manager.

COMPETITIVE TENDER see TRADITIONAL CONTRACTING

CONSORTIA

A consortium is the grouping together of three or more organisations, generally or differing skills, with the objective of carrying out a specific project.

CONTINUITY TENDER

A continuity tender is similar to the serial tender. Contractors competitively tendering for a project are informed that given satisfactory performance, they will be awarded a similar project to follow on from the completion of the first and that the price for this will be negotiated, possibly using the prices of the original bill.

CONSTRUCTION MANAGEMENT (CM)

Construction management or CM is the term used in the USA to describe management contracting. (See also professional construction management.)

COST REIMBURSEMENT see FIXED FEE/PRIME COST CONTRACT

DESIGN-BUILD

Design-build or design-construct is where the contractor provides the design and construction under one contract.

DESIGN-CONSTRUCT see DESIGN-BUILD

FAST TRACKING

Fast tracking is a means of reducing project time by the overlapping of design and construction. Each trade's work commences as its plans and specifications are substantially completed.

FIXED FEE/PRIME COST CONTRACT

Under this arrangement the contractor carries out the work for the payment of a prime cost (defined) and a fixed fee calculated in relation to the estimated amount of the prime cost.

FIXED PRICE CONTRACT

A fixed price contract may be a lump sum contract or a measurement contract based on fixed prices for units of specific work.

JOINT VENTURE

A joint venture is the pooling of the asscts and liabilities of two or more firms for the purpose of accomplishing a specific goal and on the basis of sharing profits/losses.

LUMP SUM CONTRACT

With a lump sum contract, the contractor agrees to perform the work for one fixed price, regardless of the ultimate cost.

MANAGEMENT CONTRACTING

With management contracting the contractor works alongside the design and cost consultants, providing a construction management service on a number of professional bases. The management contractor does not undertake either design or direct construction work. The design requirements are met by letting each element of the construction to specialist sub-contractors.

MANAGEMENT FEE see MANAGEMENT CONTRACTING

NEGOTIATED CONTRACT

In a negotiated contract the client selects, at the outset, one main contractor with whom to negotiate. In essence the arrangement is the same as that for a two-stage tender.

PACKAGE DEAL

A package deal follows the same lines as design-build, with the contractor providing the design and construction under one contract, but there is the implication that the building provided will be of a standardised or semi-standardised type.

PROCUREMENT

Procurement is the amalgam of activities undertaken by the client to obtain a building.

PROFESSIONAL CONSTRUCTION MANAGEMENT

PCM is a term used in the USA to describe an arrangement whereby the tasks of planning, design and construction are integrated by a project team comprising the owner, construction manager and the design organisation.

PROFESSIONAL CONSTRUCTION MANAGER (PCM) or CONSTRUCTION MANAGER

The PCM acts as a management contractor (UK) specialising in construction management within the professional construction management concept.

PROJECT MANAGEMENT

Project management is concerned with the overall planning and co-ordination of a project from inception to completion aimed at meeting the client's requirements and ensuring completion on time, within cost and to required quality standards.

SEPARATE CONTRACTS

With separate contracts the client's professional adviser let contracts for the work with a number of separate contractors. This arrangement was commonplace prior to the emergence of the general contractor.

SERIAL TENDER

A serial tender is where a number of similar projects are awarded to a contractor, following a competitive tender on a master bill of quantities. This master bill forms a standing offer open for the client to accept for a number of contracts. Each contract is separate and the price for each calculated separately.

TARGET COST CONTRACT

This form of cost reimbursable contract involves the fixing of a cost either for the complete project or in respect of certain elements only, eg labour, or materials, or plant. If the final cost deviates from the target, the saving or excess is divided between client and contractor in pre-determined proportions.

TRADITIONAL CONTRACTING

The traditional form of contracting is where the client appoints an architect or other professional to produce the design, select the contractor and to supervise the work through to completion. The contractor is selected on some basis of competition.

TURNKEY

A turnkey contract is one where the client has an agreement with one single administrative entity, who provides the design and construction under one contract, and frequently effects land acquisition, financing, leasing, etc.

TWO-STAGE TENDER

With a two-stage tender three or four contractors with appropriate experience are separately involved in detailed discussions with the client's professional advisers regarding all aspects of the project. Price competition is introduced through an approximate or notional bill or schedule of rates. Further selection criteria are then used to determine which contractor carries out the job.

ABBREVIATIONS

ACA	Association of Consultant Architects
BEC	Building Employers Confederation
BPF	British Property Federation
CD 81	JCT Standard form of building contract with contractor's design, 1981 edition
CIOB	Chartered Institute of Building
IFC 84	JCT Intermediate form of building contract, 1984 edition
JCT	Joint Contracts Tribunal
JCT 80	JCT Standard form of building contract, 1980 edition
MC 87	JCT Standard form of management contract
NEDO	National Economic Development Office
PSA	Property Services Agency
RIBA	Royal Institute of British Architects
RICS	Royal Institution of Chartered Surveyors
RICS JO (QS)	RICS Junior Organisation (Quantity Surveyors' Division)

PREFACE

The primary purpose of this publication is to provide a guide for clients of the building industry and their advisers to the various contractual arrangements which have evolved during the 1970s and 80s for the procurement of buildings.

Figure 1 indicates the alternative types of 'system' and some of the terms in current usage. The glossary provides a more comprehensive guide to the terms.

Much of the text is concerned with so called *fast-track* alternatives to the traditional client – architect – contractor selected by competitive contractual arrangement. The essence of fast-track arrangements is over-lapping the design and construction stages as a means of reducing project time.

Section 3 contains a case-study of the time and cost effects of carrying out a commercial project using traditional and fast-track contractual arrangements.

Figure 9 demonstrates the time-saving and commercial advantages of the fast-track approach. The construction cost is shown to be £0.5 million *more* if the fast-track approach is used yet by the end of month 24 the total project cost of the fast-track approach is almost £2 million *less* than the project which adopted the traditional contractual arrangements. In many respects this is the most significant aspect of alternative procurement systems.

The operation and characteristics of the alternative systems are discussed in section 2, with section 4 providing a basis for their comparison. Selecting the most appropriate procurement path is largely a matter of determining which of the client's performance requirements head the list of priorities.

Other sections are concerned with the incidence of use of the systems, with clients' needs and expectations of project organisations and with a brief review of systems in Europe.

For the serious student of building procurement systems the bibliography provides an extensive source of reference.

1. INTRODUCTION

Background to change

Until the 1960s a client with a need for building works would usually commission an architect to prepare drawings identifying his requirements. These drawings would provide the basis for competitive tenders by builders for the execution of the works. It is a system which was established early in the 19th century and which has continued for more than a century and a half. It is customarily referred to as the 'traditional system', or just 'traditional'.

In seeking an answer to why alternatives to the traditional system have evolved one might start with Sir Harold Emmerson who was asked by the Minister in 1962 to make a quick review of the problems facing the construction industry.[1] His report included the now famous phrase that:

'in no other important industry is the responsibility for design so far removed from the responsibility for production'.

He concluded that the client suffered as a result of this divorce'.

Emmerson's report led to the formation of the Banwell Committee[2] a year or so later which recommended a number of changes in contract procedures. The changes were, in themselves, significant but the most important effect of the Banwell Report was the change it engendered in the attitudes of central and local government. At that time some 60% of the construction industry's work was commissioned by central and local government. They were the industry's major clients and were in a strong position to dictate the contractual arrangements to be adopted.

Furthermore, the existence of a government commissioned report, which encouraged government departments and local authorities to consider alternative approaches to building procurement, made them less liable to charges of misconduct, failure to obtain the lowest tender etc etc. The relevant departments were able to take a wider view of public accountability; a view which was concerned not just with which tender submitted in competition was the lowest but which contractual arrangement facilitated the optimum overall result.

Most of the new arrangements claimed to facilitate shorter project periods, making earlier occupation possible and allowing the client to obtain an earlier return on his investment. The winds of change had started to blow through the construction industry!

The key issues identified by Banwell were:

- those who spend money on construction work seldom give enough attention at the start to defining their own requirements and preparing a programme

1

of events for meeting them. Insufficient regard is paid to the importance of time and its proper use;

- as the complexity of construction work increases, the need to form a design team at the outset, with all those participating in the design as full members, becomes vital;

- design and construction are no longer two separate fields and there are occasions when the main contractor should join the team at an early stage. The relationship between those responsible for design and those who actually build must be improved through common education;

- some measure of selective tendering is preferable to 'open' tendering: impediments should be removed and rules for the conduct of selective tendering drawn up for the guidance of local authorities;

- the use of unorthodox methods of appointing the contractor, where appropriate, has advantages which should not be lost to members of the public sector through adherence to outmoded procedures;

- serial tenders offer great possibilities for continuity of employment; the development of experienced production teams, etc and the banding together of those who have suitable work in prospect is to be encouraged;

- negotiated contracts need not be rigidly excluded in the public field; methods of contracting should be examined for the value of the solutions they offer to problems rather than for their orthodoxy.

Notwithstanding the stimulus that the Banwell report gave to change there were two other over-riding factors:

- the failure of the construction industry to satisfy the client's needs, particularly in respect of its management of exceptionally large and complex projects;

- high inflation, coupled with high borrowing rates, which led to shorter project periods becoming of great importance to clients, particularly those who required an early return on their investment in property if the project was to be viable.

During the period 1973–74 many of the oil-producing states combined to bring about massive increases in the price of crude oil. The outcome was immediate, with massive increases in the borrowing rate and in inflation. The economy of the Western World was in disarray. A disarray which continued for more than a decade.

1. Introduction

The increase in the public's and the construction industry's interest in alternative ways of procuring buildings more quickly was most marked following the oil crisis, as the industry's clients and their advisers realised that for many projects time was now of the essence.

There is little doubt that there was a positive relationship between the increase in borrowing rates subsequent to the oil crisis and the construction industry's interest in alternative system of building procurement.

The cost effect of undertaking the design stage in parallel with the construction stage is demonstrated in the case study in Section 3. Parallel working can produce significant reductions in the total cost of a project. These reductions are particularly pronounced when interest rates are high and when obtaining a return on investment made in the project is an important feature.

The growth of alternative systems for the procurement of buildings has had a significant effect on the role of the builder. His horizons are now wider. Previously, his activities were confined to carrying out the works. Now the builder is engaged as a management contractor, construction manager, as a member of a design-and-build team, or as a project manager and is able to work with members of the design team and advise the client on aspects of buildability which may have time and cost implications and so improve the overall viability of the project to the client's advantage.

2. PROCUREMENT SYSTEMS

Alternative systems, types and terms

Figure 1 illustrates the various sytems which have evolved. The four principal types of system are:

- designer-led competitive tender;

- designer-led construction works managed for fee;

- package deal;

- project manager/client's representative-led.

Various terms have emerged to identify the systems in current use, some of which are shown in Figure 1.

The project manager/client's representative-led arrangement may be used in conjunction with any of the others.

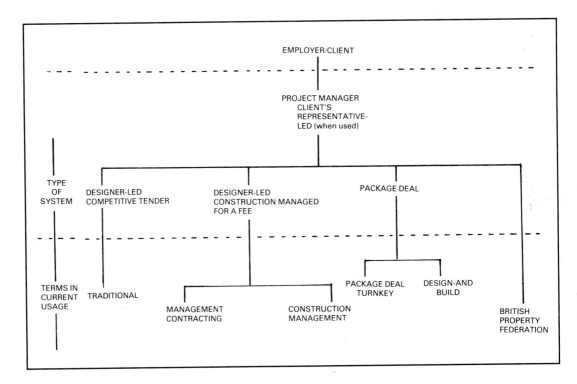

Figure 1 Systems for building procurement

DESIGNER-LED COMPETITIVE TENDER

Because most clients for construction work seek, at first, someone who can express their needs in the form of a design, the designer is, traditionally, the leader of the construction process. This 'traditional' approach provides a useful datum for consideration of the other systems available.

Traditional system

The traditional system has evolved and developed over the centuries. The role of the architect was established in more or less its present form by the end of the 18th century by which time he was recognised as the independent designer of buildings and manager of the construction process.

Early in the 19th century bills of quantities began to be used as the means of providing a number of different contractors with a common basis for tendering. By the middle of the century the quantity surveyor was established as an independent compiler of bills of quantities and an expert in building accounts and cost matters.

There is considerable evidence, extending back over several centuries, of building craftsmen acting as contractors for complete building projects embracing the work of all crafts. Nevertheless, the general contractor in his present form is frequently regarded as coming into his own at the beginning of the 19th century.

The present traditional system which involves the parties mentioned above is enshrined in the Standard Form of Building Contract (with quantities).

Extent of use

There are no reliable figures of the extent of use of the system but indications are that, perhaps, 60% to 70% of building projects, by value of the works, adopt the traditional system.

Operation

The components of the traditional approach may be seen in a simplified form in Figure 2. The process starts, as for all such processes, with a client having a need for a building (nodes ① – ②).

He briefs his architect on his needs, as he sees them, and by node ③ the cost ceiling for the project has been decided. The quantity surveyor should have provided preliminary cost advice by this stage.

Between nodes ③ and ④ the architect prepares alternative drawings/ proposals so that the client may select that which he prefers; the quantity surveyor estimates the cost of the alternatives.

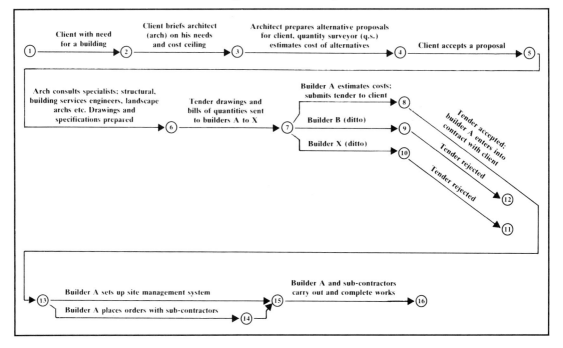

Figure 2 The 'traditional' system (using standard form of building contract with quantities

Between nodes ④ and ⑤ the client accepts a proposal.

Between nodes ⑤ and ⑥ the architect develops the design of the accepted proposal. This will probably entail consultations with specialist engineers and negotiations with specialist contractors.

Drawings and specifications are prepared and the quantity surveyor provides regular monitoring of the alternative designs to ensure that the cost implications of the design decisions are known to all concerned. The quantity surveyor prepares bills of quantities.

Between nodes ⑥ and ⑦ , tender drawings, bills of quantities and forms of tender are sent to selected builders (contractors) in order that they may submit tenders for the work.

Beyond node ⑦ the builders estimate the costs of the operations involved in the project. The duration of the project is assessed from the pre-tender plan prepared by the builders' production planners and managers. Management decisions determine the margin to be added to the tender for profit.

In Figure 2 the tender submitted by Builder A is accepted by the client and he and the builder enter into a contract (nodes ⑧ – ⑬). The other tenders are rejected (nodes ⑨ – ⑫)and ⑩ – ⑪).

Between nodes ⑬ and ⑮, Builder A, sets up his site management system, plans and organises the works, schedules materials' deliveries etc. Concurrently, Builder A places orders with his own sub-contractors and those nominated by the architect (nodes ⑬ — ⑭).

Between nodes ⑮ and ⑯ Builder A and the sub-contractors carry out and complete the works.

Characteristics of the system

- The system has operated in Britain, the Commonwealth and other parts of the world reasonably satisfactorily. It has stood the test of time.

- It is understood by most clients and they know their financial commitment when they accept the builder's tender, if the design has been fully developed at time of going to tender.

- The architect has considerable freedom to conceive and develop the design without excessive time or economic pressures, provided the cost ceiling is not exceeded and the client's requirements are generally satisfied.

- The project cost can be estimated, planned and monitored by the quantity surveyor from inception stage through to completion of the project.

- The system makes it possible for the architect to introduce consulting engineers, landscape architects and other experts to advise on or design 'sub-systems' of the project. $\overset{\frown}{A}$ 6

- The architect is able to consult specialist contractors and suppliers who he believes to be appropriate for the project or who manufacture and/or install components for sub-systems which would be compatible with the system as a whole at design stage, with a view to nominating them subsequently as sub-contractors or suppliers for the project. A

- Sub-contractors may be invited to submit competitive tenders to the architect for the sub-system in which they specialise, thus ensuring that the most economic price is obtained. A 7

- Drawings and bills of quantities provide a common basis for competitive tenders from selected main contractors. A 5.

- In the event of the client requiring the project to be varied during the course of construction, the bills of quantities contain prices for items of work which may be used to adjust the contract sum to take into account the variation(s). A 8

- The design should be fully developed before bills of quantities and, subsequently, tenders are prepared. If not, excessive variations and disruption of the works are likely to occur.

- The need for the design to be fully developed before tenders are prepared leads to an 'end-on' design/build arrangement. Frequently, such an arrangement requires a longer overall project period than is necessary if both design and construction are able to proceed concurrently.

- As the length of the project period increases so does the project cost, because the client usually incurs financing charges on the sum which he has invested in land purchase, interim payments to the contractor and other members of the building team.

- Many contractors are of the opinion that their ability to organise and control the work of nominated sub-contractors is undermined by the nomination process, because such sub-contractors have less loyalty to the contractor than to the architect who nominated them.

- The separation of the design and construction processes tends to foster a 'them and us' attitude between the designers and contractors. This reduces the team spirit that experience has shown to be vital for the satisfactory conclusion of a building project.

- Lines of communication between the parties tend to be tenuous and the interests of all may suffer as a consequence.

- The traditional systems has been proved to be unsatisfactory for some large and complex projects which require advanced management systems, structures and skills.

Standard forms of contract

JCT80 and IFC 84 may both be used with quantities and are appropriate for the traditional system.

Standard forms of sub-contracts are used for nominated sub-contracts under JCT 80 and for named sub-contracts under IFC 84.

The standard domestic (DOM) form of sub-contract is used with both JCT 80 and IFC 84.

Fast-track

The term 'fast-track' has been more subject to varying definitions than others but overlapping of design and construction as a means of reducing project time is a generally recognised characteristic of the term. This overlapping, often referred to as 'parallel working', can be achieved by using a modified version of the traditional system or by adopting a form of construction management or management contracting.

DESIGNER-LED, CONSTRUCTION WORKS MANAGED FOR A FEE

Under this heading are included the various management fee and construction management systems. There are almost as many variations on different systems as there are firms offering management services. The vast majority of the variations have one feature in common; the management contractor or construction manager offers to undertake the management of the works for a fee. He is, in effect, in much the same relationship with the client as is the architect or any other consultant. The actual construction work is undertaken by specialist contractors, each of whom contracts to carry out and complete one or more of the work packages which make up the whole of the works.

Those firms who adopt the title management contractor are normally those which are divisions of major construction contractor companies. One or two management contractors are now concerned solely with management contracting, having abandoned their original, traditional, contractor activities. The management contractor almost invariably employs the specialist contractors who undertake the work packages as his sub-contractors. It is the employment of the specialist contractors which typically distinguishes the management contractor from the construction manager. When a construction manager firm is employed the specialist contractors are generally in direct contract with the client, rather than being sub-contractors to the construction manager.

It is not possible to make categorical statements regarding who employs the specialist contractors (client or managing firm), because there are no codes of practice governing the operation of these contractual arrangements, but the broad generalisations made may be taken as a reliable guide.

Two-stage tendering

Two-stage tendering or two-tier tendering is another version of management contracting.

A statistically insignificant number of architectural firms adopt a successful variation of the construction management approach, the principal proponents being Moxley, Jenner and Partners. They refer to the approach as Alternative Method of Management (AMM). The client enters into separate contracts with the specialist contractors. The architect employs the site manager and undertakes responsibility for construction in addition to design.

The fee the contractor or construction manager, as the case may be, receives for undertaking management is not usually directly related to the value of the work being managed. It is not, for example, a percentage of the work value. In this way it cannot be said that the contractor has anything to gain if the value of work increases. The fee would, however, be renegotiated if the extent of the works changed significantly.

Management contracting/construction management

The best known example of management/fee contracting in Britain is the Bovis system. Bovis have operated fee systems, notably with Marks and Spencer as a client, for more than 60 years with proven success. Very few other contractors operated such a system before the 1960s but management contracting is now well established as a procurement path.

Extent of use

A significant percentage of major building projects particularly those in South East of England, adopt a 'fee' system of procurement. Nationally, however, probably no more than 10%, by value of the work, adopt a fee system. The use of this procurement approach appears to be declining but for major projects management for a fee systems have a considerable following of 'repeat' clients, regardless of statistical trends.

There is evidence that despite the overall decline in use, fee contracts are being adopted in some cities in the Midlands and the North where they had seldom if ever been used in the past.

Operation

The process of a typical management contracting system is shown in Figure 3. The construction manager's role is similar to that of the management contractor but he is less likely to be appointed by competitive tender. When a construction manager is appointed the works package contractors will most usually be in direct contract with the client.

For practical purposes 'construction manager' may be read for 'builder', 'contractor', and 'management contractor' in the following text under this heading, and in Figure 3.

It must be emphasised that the following 'operation' notes should be regarded as merely indicative of such systems.

Referring to Figure 3 it can be seen that between nodes ① and ⑤ the system is similar to that of the traditional system.

Between nodes ⑤ and ⑥, however, the architect and quantity surveyor concentrate on preparing drawings and a 'Preliminaries' bill of quantities in sufficient detail to enable the prospective fee contractor(s) to determine the method to be used for construction and to prepare a firm fee tender. At the same time the architect and other members of the design team develop the design generally and prepare drawings and specifications.

Beyond node ⑥ the contractor, (or contractors if the client seeks competitive tenders), prepares the first stage tender for the management fee. It is unusual for more than two or three contractors to be invited to tender.

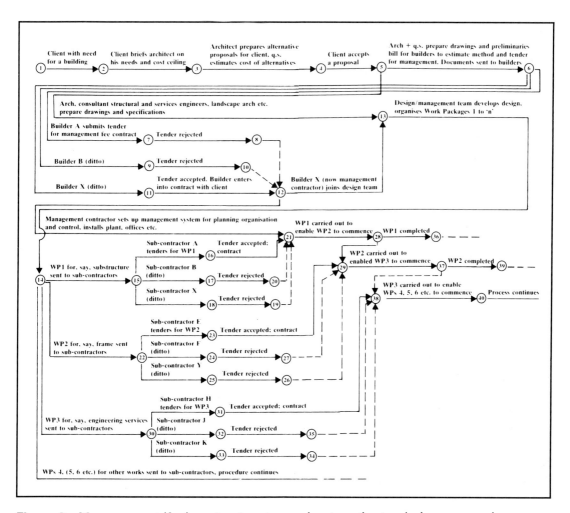

Figure 3   Management (fee) contract system using two-tier tendering approach

By the time node ⑫ is reached Contractor X enters into a fee contract with the client and the other tenders are rejected.

The most competitive tender is often regarded as of less importance than a credible construction programme and a sound track record.

Extensive interviews with the staff of the contractors who are tendering are usually regarded by client and design team as an essential aspect of the selection process. This ensures compatibility between design team and contractor's staff who will, if the tender is accepted, be working closely together as design and management team.

Between nodes ⑫ and ⑬ the management contractor, as he has now become, joins the design team. Concurrently, (nodes ⑫ to ㉑), he establishes a management system for planning, organising and controlling the project. He instals the plant, site offices etc.

Between nodes ⑫ and ⑬ the design/management team continues to develop the design and organises a series of work packages for all aspects of the work. The work packages provide the basis for a number of contracts which are placed as soon as the necessary information is available.

Beyond node ⑭ the work packages are put out to tender and contracts entered into. Drawings and bills of quantities or specifications may be used as the documentation for the sub-contract tenders. Between thirty and forty work packages is by no means unusual. For major projects the number of work packages may be as many as one hundred and fifty.

The works contained in the work packages are frequently commenced almost as soon as the contracts have been placed. Project completion is achieved with completion of all the work packages.

Characteristics of the system

- Management contracting has been used successfully to a limited extent since the 1920's and with increasing frequency during the 1970's and 1980's.

- Clients and contractors often adopt the system on a regular basis once they have gained experience, which suggests that it has merits. It is generally recognised that its adoption requires mutual trust.

- Work can commence as soon as design proposals have been accepted by the client and drawings have been approved by the local authority.

- The management contractor (or construction manager) is appointed much earlier than would be possible with the traditional system. He is able to become a member of the design team and contribute his construction knowledge and management expertise.

- Management contractors (or construction managers) frequently compete at first stage tender ensuring that an economical fee is charged for management.

- 'Them and us' attitudes are reduced and lines of communication are improved.

- The management contractor finds it easier to identify with the client's needs and interests and 'integration of the team' becomes possible and practical.

- Decisions regarding appointment of sub-contractors are made jointly (by designers and construction manager or management contractor), thus making use of wider experience.

- Specialist (or sub-contractors) compete at second stage tender ensuring economical tenders.

- Contracts are entered into near the time of commencement of the works making firm-price tenders possible.

- Tenders submitted near the time of commencement of work are frequently more competitive than those submitted several months or even years ahead.

- When a construction manager is employed the client enters into contracts with numerous specialist contractors instead of with a general contractor as would be the case if the traditional system were adopted. He usually has a closer involvement in the project throughout its whole life.

- Lines of communication between clients and specialist contractors are shorter than with the traditional system. Advantages which stem from this factor are:

    the client is enabled to make prompt decisions which can be implemented without delay; it makes possible a prompt response by the client to unforeseen site problems and by the contractor to changes required by the client;

    the cost implications of design changes can be promptly assessed and cost control for the client is thereby facilitated.

- Specialist contractors frequently prefer to be in contract with the client rather than with a management contractor because interim payments are usually made more promptly when paid direct.

- When contracts are made direct between client and specialist contractor, conditions of contract can be adopted which are appropriate to the needs of the works to be undertaken.

- The total project completion period is reduced by parallel working.

- A reduced project completion period produces a corresponding reduction in financing charges on the sum invested in land purchase, interim payments to contractors and other members of the building team. Inflation has less effect.

- The client takes delivery of the building earlier because the project completion period is reduced. He thus obtains a return on his investment more quickly.

- The client is usually given an approximate estimate of the final project cost by the quantity surveyor and/or contractor early in the project life, but he does not know the final project cost until the last sub-contract is entered into. On other projects he is given a guaranteed maximum cost.

- The architect may have less time to develop the design because he is under greater pressure from client, contractor and sub-contractors. The design may suffer as a result.

Standard forms of contract

The JCT Standard Form of Management Contract, 1987 edition (MC 87), may be used for contracts between the employer (client) and management contractor.

Works Contracts, WC/1 and WC/2 are used for contracts between the management contractor and the various works (sub-) contractors.

PACKAGE DEAL/DESIGN AND BUILD

Under this heading are included terms such as turnkey, package deal, contractor's design and design-and-build system. To all intents and purposes the terms turnkey and package deal have the same meaning.

The range of services offered by package deal contractors varies greatly. Some will find sites, arrange mortgages, sale-and-leaseback and similar facilities, in addition to designing and building to meet the client's requirements. Others contract to design and build a unique building on the client's own site. The feature that the systems have in common is that the 'contractor' is responsible for the whole of the design and construction of the building. Responsibilities are not split between designer and builder so that the client finds himself looking to separate 'parties' in the event of a building failure. The systems offer 'single-point responsibility', a feature that commends itself to clients frustrated by the traditional system.

Package deal contracts involve direct negotiation between client and contractor (or several contractors if the client seeks competitive tenders). The client states his requirements and the contractor (or contractors) prepares design and cost proposals to meet the requirements. Initially, the contractor produces only sufficient by way of design proposals to demonstrate his 'package' to the client. The design is fully developed when both parties have reached an agreement regarding specification and price.

Experience indicates that clients are frequently able to procure buildings more quickly when these contractual arrangements are adopted. Time savings tend to go hand-in-hand with cost savings.

Design-and-build is a more refined form of package deal which obtained recognition from the Joint Contracts Tribunal in 1981 with the publication of the JCT Standard Form of Building Contract with Contractor's Design (CD 81). This recognition followed changes in British architects' codes of practice which allowed architects to become directors of construction firms. Hitherto, they were able to be salaried employees but director status had been denied. Figure 4 shows the stages in the operation of CD 81.

There is evidence that package-deal design standards have improved as architects have taken up senior appointments in design-and-build firms or, as is by no means unusual, founded firms which are predominantly designer-led.

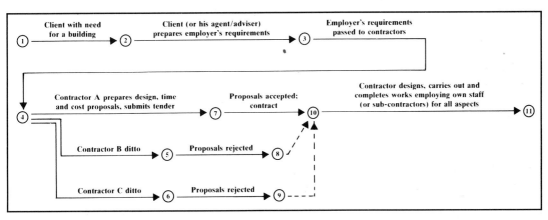

Figure 4   Design and build system

Most types of building have been constructed using a package deal approach but industrial and office buildings in new development areas are the most typical examples of building types which are frequently built using a package deal system. Many package deals involve a proprietary building system of one sort or another. Package dealers frequently advertise their services and/or product in the pages of newspapers and journals read by the people who are likely to make decisions regarding their firm's future building needs. Package deals provide buildings rather than designs and the dealer may offer to find a site in the part of the country where, for example, government grants are available to the client, in order that he has an incentive to expand his business in that area – high unemployment areas, for example.

The package dealer will usually undertake to obtain planning permission and building regulations approvals.

Extent of use

It has been estimated that between 15% and 20% of building projects, by value of work, are carried out by some form of package deal. The use of this procurement approach appears to be increasing.

Operation

For purposes of illustration the contractual arrangement and terms used in CD 81 have been used.

The components of the system may be seen in Figure 4. It starts when the client identifies his need for a building between nodes ① and ② , and states his requirements between nodes ③ and ④ . In practice he may ask an 'agent' to prepare his 'Employer's Requirements', as they are termed in CD 81. The client might employ an architect, quantity surveyor, building surveyor or similar competent person to state his requirements but such a person's task would be complete when he had prepared the statement.

The client's requirements are passed to the design-and-build contractors, nodes ③ to ④ , each of which prepares a design and ascertains the time it will take to carry out the works. At the same time he prepares an estimate of the cost of his 'proposals' and submits a tender, (following node ④). No more detail is given than is necessary for tender purposes.

The client's requirements need to be submitted only in sufficient detail to enable the contractors to ascertain needs and submit their proposals. In Figure 4 three contractors are shown to be submitting proposals but it is by no means unusual for a client to negotiate with only one contractor.

In Figure 4 the proposals of Contractors 'B' and 'C' are rejected but those of Contractor 'A' are accepted, (between nodes ⑤ and ⑩). Contractor 'A' now prepares a detailed design and carries out and completes the works employing his own staff or sub-contractors.

The contractor's proposals normally include a 'Contract Sum Analysis', which takes the place of bills of quantities. It is generally accepted that the Contract Sum Analysis should contain sufficient pricing data to enable the cost of 'changes in the Employer's Requirements' to be calculated, should changes occur.

There is provision in CD 81 for the client to nominate an 'employer's agent' whose role is to receive or issue applications, consents, instructions, notices, requests or statements or to otherwise act for the employer. This agent will probably, but not necessarily, be the man who prepared the statement of client's requirements. He has a much more restricted role than that enjoyed by the architect or supervising officer when the traditional system is used.

Characteristics of the system

- It is used increasingly as a means of managing the building process at home and abroad.

- It provides single point responsibility so that in the event of a building failure the contractor is solely responsible. There can be no question of 'passing the buck' between architect and builder as has so often been the case in the past. The client's interests are safeguarded in this respect.

- The client knows his total financial commitment early in the project's life, provided he does not introduce changes during the course of the works.

- The client has direct contact with the contractor. This improves lines of communication and enables the contractor to respond and to adapt more promptly to the client's needs.

- The contractor is responsible for design, construction planning, organisation and control. These activities can proceed concurrently to a greater extent than is generally possible using the traditional system.

- The package dealer may provide a comprehensive package comprising site seeking and purchase, obtaining planning permission and building regulations approval, financing facilities, leasing etc.

- The package dealer may use a proprietary building system or modular building form which reduces design time and the time required for approval of the building components.

- The client is frequently able to see examples of the package dealer's product when his proposals are being made. Most clients can visualise their needs more readily in three dimensions (by moving within and 'sampling' an actual building) than by the study of drawings and specifications. Quality, a feature which it is difficult to specify, may be more easily indicated by comparison with a sample.

- Many systems used by package dealers have been tested over a period of years and are less prone to teething troubles.

- There have been some serious failures among building systems.

- The package dealer's components are often readily available so that manufacturing time is minimal and construction time may be correspondingly reduced because manufacture of components and work on site can proceed concurrently.

- Work on the building can commence as soon as local authority approvals have been obtained and sufficient information regarding the earlier site operations is available. The design does not need to be finalised before some, at least, of the work may be commenced.

- The package dealer is familiar with the construction methods to be used for his product and work proceeds more quickly.

- Some proprietary package deal products lack aesthetic appeal.

- The range of designs which is available from some proprietary package dealers is sometimes limited.

- Competition between the contractor's proposals should ensure economical tenders and alternative design concepts.

- The relaxation of the architects' code of practice makes it possible for them to become full partners in design-and-build firms.

- This relaxation should lead to the construction of buildings which reflect the senior status of the designer in the team and lead to more aesthetically pleasing buildings than may have been built in some instances in the past.

- The nature of the system should promote the creation of an integrated design and construction team.

- The closer involvement of architects in the building process should lead to designs which have a greater appreciation of construction methods; 'buildability'.

- The integrated nature of the team improves communication between designer and builder which encourages prompt decisions.

- A prompt response is achieved in the event of materials or manpower shortages.

- Design costs are built into the package but because the design input and 'detailing' required are less than when using the traditional system the costs involved are frequently less.

- There is no independent architect or similar 'professional' available to the client to advise on the technical quality of the designs at time of tender, although he is not precluded from seeking such advice if he so wishes.

- The employer's agent may supervise the works and ensure that the contractor's proposals are complied with and that the work is not skimped.

- The nature of the contract tends to reduce changes (variations) from the original design and disruption of the works is less likely to occur.

- The reduction of changes and disruption produces time and cost savings which benefit the client.

- The total project completion period is reduced.

- Time savings reduce the employer's financing charges, inflation has less effect and the building is operational sooner which, in a commercial context, produces an earlier return on the capital invested.

Standard forms of contract

CD 81 is intended for use on projects where the client provides the site which is the subject of the contract. Many design-and-build projects use conditions of contract drafted for specific purposes. The diverse nature of these projects leads to corresponding diverse conditions of contract.

DOM forms of sub-contract may be used between contractor and the various sub-contractors.

PROJECT MANAGER/CLIENT'S REPRESENTATIVE

During the 1960s and 1970s construction projects tended to become larger and more complex. It became apparent that the time-honoured client-architect-builder relationship was sometimes inadequate as a system for constructing buildings within cost-budgets and tight time-schedules. There was a need for someone to manage the project as a separate, distinct member of the construction team – a project manager or client's representative.

There is nothing new in the concept of a project manager. Before the end of the 17th century when architecture, as a profession, was established in Britain, virtually all major building projects for Church and Crown – the principal clients of the building industry – were designed by craftsmen and managed by influential 'clerks' who were frequently known as Clerk of Works or Masters of Works.

These men were the client's representative. They held the pursestrings and they had overall management of the project. The emergence of project managers for major projects in the 1960s marked the return to a system which existed for some six hundred years in Britain.

The essence of the appointment of a project manager or client's representative is that a single person acts as surrogate client. The title project manager is that which is most generally employed but client's representative is becoming increasingly used. Whichever title is used the role is to ensure that all the needs of the client are satisfied and to act as the contact point between client and the building procurement team. It is the direct relationship between client (whose interest the project manager represents), and the project manager which distinguishes his role from other 'managers' in the construction process who frequently have the word 'project' affixed to their 'manager' title.

The Wood Report[3] suggests that the project manager's prime task is one of co-ordinating client requirements such that clear instructions from a single source can be provided to the other parties involved. The importance of the client identifying a single person to represent his interests (before he has a firm commitment to actually building), and to assist him with drafting the brief for the project is recognised in *Thinking about building*,[4] which provides a guide to the selection of the most appropriate procurement path to meet a potential client's specific needs.

A vital feature of the project manager's/client's representative's role is that he is concerned solely with managing the project. Because he is not involved in designing or constructing the building works he is able to take an objective overview of the activities of all concerned.

In 1988 the NEDO report *Faster building for commerce*[5] identified the need for the client, (referred to in the report as the 'customer') to appoint an experienced 'customer representative' with experience in working with the construction industry if his in-house project executive was insufficiently experienced. The report suggested that such a person can be found among architects, engineers, surveyors, project managers or in contracting companies with management and/or design skills as well as those of construction.

Such a representative must have sufficient status and authority to act on the client's behalf in the dialogue between the client's organisation and the team appointed to procure the building. There is no reason to believe that the requirements of clients for commercial buildings differ greatly from those of clients for other types of building.

2. Procurement Systems

The relationship between the parties to the contract when a project manager or client's/customer's representative is employed is shown in Figure 5.

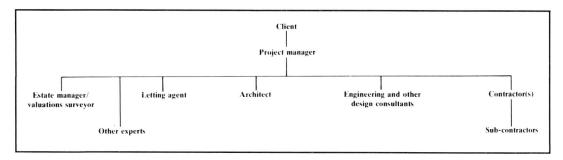

Figure 5   Relationship between parties for project management systems

Extent of use

Project managers have been engaged with increasing frequency and success during the 1970s and 1980s but there is no record of the extent of use.

Operation

The components of the system may be seen in Figure 6. As with the systems described previously there is a client with a need for a building. Between nodes ② and ③ a project manager is engaged.

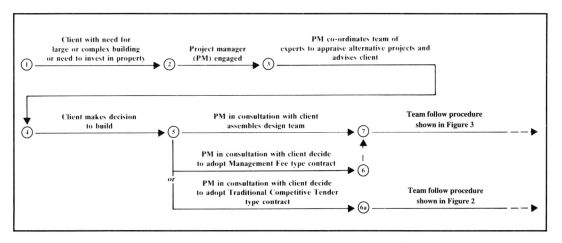

Figure 6   Project management

The first task of the project manager is to appraise alternative ways of meeting the client's needs; (nodes ③ to ④). If, for example, the aim of the project is to maximise the client's return on his investment, the project manager might well consult letting agents or undertake extensive market research. On high technology projects, such as nuclear power stations, the appraisal might be between alternative energy sources. The magnitude of many projects requiring the engagement of a project manager is such that his task at this stage would be as 'co-ordinator of expertise'. He would then present the experts' collective recommendations to the client for his decision regarding the project which best suited his needs, (between nodes ④ and ⑤). In practice the client would more usually be the board of directors of a corporation or the council of a public authority.

Nodes ④ to ⑤ mark the point at which a decision has to be made regarding the selection of the contracting system to be employed. If some form of management fee system is to be employed the contractor may be appointed at this stage. In this event he will join the design team and the remarks made about this system will apply.

Between nodes ⑤ and ⑦ the project manager assembles the design team which will best suit the project's special features, whilst at the same time endeavouring to appoint people who will work well together. An appreciation of the human aspects of management is an important part of the project manager's skills. Beyond node ⑥ or ⑥a the project is designed, costed and constructed. It is important that the cost implications of design variables are ascertained as promptly as possible so that their effect on project viability can be considered by the project team and appropriate action taken.

If the contractor has not been selected at node ⑥ , nor joined the design team at that point, he may be selected beyond node ⑥a by competition, using the traditional system.

Alternatively, a package deal contractor may be appointed. In which event the project manager's role would be mainly concerned with acting on the client's behalf in the dialogue between his organisation and the contractor.

Characteristics of the system

- It has been used with increasing frequency and success during the 1970s and 1980s for complex and large projects.

- It is popular because of the dissatisfaction of some clients with the traditional system and its associated delays and excessive costs.

- The project manager is a 'professional', surrogate, client with experience of identifying and stating the client's needs and requirements.

- A project manager will often have a professional background appropriate to the type of building to be constructed.

- The project manager is able to act as a leader who can take into account all aspects of the project; finance, feasibility, design and time and hold a balance between them.

- The engagement of a project manager releases the client from the need to delegate a member of his staff (often a member without previous experience) to act as the intermediary between client and project team.

- The management function is separated so that the manager is able to act in an independent capacity.

- The client incurs an additional cost from the project manager's fee but this cost is offset to some extent by savings in his own 'management' involvement.

- The design and construction functions are separated so that those involved can act as partners on equal terms.

- 'Them and us' confrontation may be avoided as a result of this separation.

- Overall project planning and control which results from the engagement of the project manager ensure that both design and production are planned and co-ordinated to give as short an overall design and construction duration as possible.

- The architect and other consultants are released from the tasks and problems associated with managing a project, enabling them to concentrate on design matters.

- The quantity surveyor carries out cost estimating and planning and control throughout the overall project period.

- The system is able to combine the advantage of the traditional system, which is understood by most clients, with improved management methods.

- The system provides for alternative means of selecting the contractor.

- Reduction of the overall project period provides consequential cost reductions as the client is able to utilise the building, or obtain a return on his investment, more promptly.

Standard forms of contract

There is no JCT standard form of contract for the employment of a project manager. JCT 80, IFC 84, CD 81 or MC 87 may be used between client and contractor. The appropriate sub-contract forms may be used between contractor and sub-contractors.

THE BRITISH PROPERTY FEDERATION SYSTEM

The British Property Federation (BPF) is a powerful client body which has recognised the importance of the client appointing a single person to represent his interests. The BPF has done much to promote the term 'client's representative'.

In November 1983 the British Property Federation published a manual of the BPF System for building design and construction. The manual comprises ninety-nine pages of which thirty-six are appendices providing schedules of responsibilities, check-lists and proformae.

The manual excited considerable interest and criticism because it proposed radical changes to established procedures. Some members of the building team saw their traditional roles threatened.

The BPF system 'unashamedly puts the client's interests first'. It attempts 'to devise a more efficient and co-operative method of organising the whole building process . . . to the genuine advantage of everyone concerned in the total construction effort'. The reason for this enterprise is that 'to build in this country costs too much, takes too long and does not always produce credible results'.

The BPF represents substantial commercial property interests and thus it was able to exercise considerable influence on the building industry and its allied professions, particularly at a time when the industry was working at much less than its optimum capacity.

The BPF manual is the only document of its kind which sets out the operation of a system in such detail. Clearly, the manual provides the definitive document and the 'operation' described below should be regarded simply as an introduction to the system. This disclaimer is significant because the manual is at pains to offer a system which can be used with various methods of contracting and one which 'although consisting of a series of precisely described steps, can be used flexibly'. In many respects the system is an amalgam of those discussed above.

Extent of use

The use of this procurement approach is increasing but measured by value of work, the system's contribution to the building industry's output is not great. Nevertheless, the system has made a significant contribution to developing the industry's attitudes and approaches to building procurement.

Operation

The components of the system may be seen in simplified form in Figure 7. The process commences at node ①, when a client plans to build.

BPF members are largely 'commercial' but the Federation's system should be capable of adoption by a wider range of clients.

The manual suggests that the client should explore the many courses open to him 'at minimal cost' and appoint a 'client's representative', who is defined as 'the person or firm responsible for managing the project on behalf of and in the interests of the client'. The client's representative may be an employee of the client or an architect, chartered surveyor, engineer or project manager.

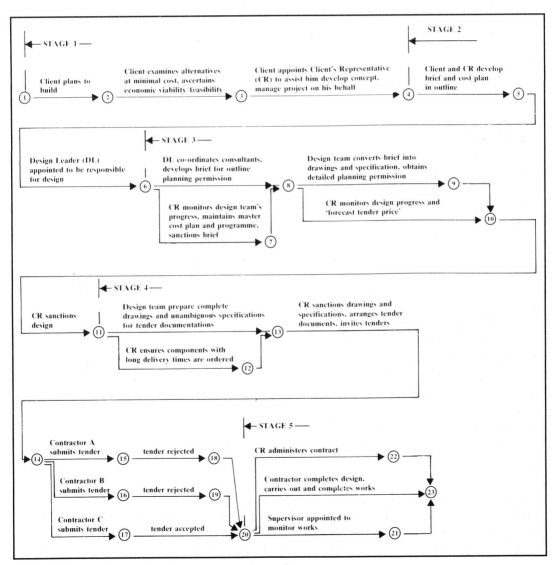

Figure 7   BPF system for building design and construction

At node ③ the client appoints the client's representative whose first tasks are to help the client develop the concept and manage the project on his behalf. Obviously, the extent to which it will be necessary for the client's representative to become involved in ascertaining the economic viability and technical feasibility of the project will depend on the client's in-house skills and expertise.

Between nodes ④ and ⑤ client and client's representative develop the outline brief and the outline cost plan to the point where the client is satisfied and to the extent that the full brief may be specified. The activities between nodes ① and ④ comprise 'Stage 1 – Concept' in the BPF manual.

Node ④ sees the commencement of 'Stage 2 – Preparation of the brief'. It is possible that the 'design leader' may have been appointed in Stage 1 but if not, he will be appointed at node ⑤ .

The design leader is defined as 'the person or firm with *overall responsibility* for the pre-tender design and for sanctioning the contractor's design'. The design leader might be an individual, a multi-disciplinary firm, or he might be a consultant with specialist consultants contracted to him. The words 'overall responsibility' have been printed in italics above to emphasise the 'unique' role of the design leader.

'Stage 3 – Design Development', commences at node ⑥ . Between nodes ⑥ and ⑧ the design leader co-ordinates consultants and develops the brief to the point where an application for outline planning permission may be obtained from the local authority.

Concurrently, the client's representative monitors the design team's progress and prepares and maintains the master cost plan and the master programme. The former is 'a schedule prepared by the client's representative of the expenditure required to implement the project' and the latter is 'a schedule prepared by the client's representative of the main activities to complete the project'.

By node ⑧ the client's representative will 'sanction' the design leader's brief and, subject to obtaining outline planning permission, the design should progress to the point where an application for detailed planning permission may be obtained, (nodes ⑧ to ⑨).

The glossary of terms refers to 'sanction' as 'the process by which the client's representative successively agrees the work of the design team to ensure that it meets the requirements of the brief'. The contractor's design is similarly sanctioned by the design leader to ensure that it complies with the contract documents.

The client's representative continues to monitor design progress and at node ⑩ agrees the 'forecast tender price' which is a 'forecast made by the design leader of the likely cost of construction'. The forecast tender price forms part of the master cost plan, referred to above.

Between nodes ⑩ and ⑪, the client's representative sanctions the design as far as it is advanced at this point.

Between nodes ⑪ and ⑫ and ⑪ and ⑬ design leader and client's representative work together towards the provision of tender documentation. The design team prepares, what are referred to in the manual as 'complete drawings' but this term may be misleading if the reader is accustomed to the traditional system in which design is entirely the province of the design team. Complete drawings in the context of the BPF system means that the drawings, together with 'clear unambiguous specifications', are sufficient as a basis on which contractors might tender without 'being justified in claiming for omissions or inadequate descriptions'. The manual points out that the quality of the information will control the standard of the buildings.

Between nodes ⑬ and ⑭ the client's representative sanctions the drawings and specification, arranges tender documents and invites tenders. 'Stage 4 – Tender documents and tendering' commences at node ⑪ and is completed at node ⑳ when a tender is accepted and a contract is entered into between client and contractor.

There will probably be a need for clarification of sundry items by all concerned with the project and the prospective contractor may be required to provide further information, costs, calculations, etc. before contracts are finally exchanged.

Tender documents consist of:

– invitation to tender with its appendices;
– specifications;
– drawings;
– conditions of contract;
– bills of quantities, should the client decide to use them.

The contractors' tenders are submitted to the client's representative.

The tender should include:

– outline priced schedule of activities;
– organisation chart;
– details of personnel;
– method statement;
– list of declared sub-contractors;
– schedule of time charges.

The tender may also contain alternative proposals for the design and construction of the building.

'Stage 5 – Construction' is carried out between nodes ⑳ and ㉓). A particular feature of the BPF system is that the contractor 'completes the design, providing co-ordinated working drawings. He obtains approval of his design from statutory authorities should this be necessary and co-ordinates the work of statutory undertakers'. The building agreement between the client and the contractor states that the contractor's design is to be sanctioned by the design leader to ensure that it complies with the tender specification.

The client's representative administers the building contract, approves payments to the contractor, decides on the need for variations and issues instruction. It is he who decides if the services of the design leader should be retained during the construction stage (nodes ⑳ – ㉓). It will be appreciated that the design team tasks should have been completed by node ⑳ ; perhaps by node ⑭ .

A supervisor is appointed to monitor the works (nodes ⑳ – ㉓ ; his duties are detailed in the appendices. They are similar to those of a clerk of works but more comprehensive in their scope.

Characteristics of the system

- It was devised, almost unilaterally, by one party to the building contract – the client – so it lacks some of the compromises inherent in agreements devised by bodies such as the Joint Contracts Tribunal. It is concerned primarily with the client's interests.

- It is designed to produce good buildings more quickly and at lower costs than the traditional system.

- It is designed to change attitudes and alter the way in which members of the professions and contractors deal with one another, with a view to creating a fully motivated and co-operative building team and to removing as much as possible of the overlap of effort between designers, quantity surveyors and contractors, which is prevalent under the traditional system.

- It is designed to redefine risks and re-establish awareness of real costs by all members of the design and construction team and to eliminate practices which absorb unnecessary effort and time and obstruct progress towards completion.

- It provides for an independent 'client's representative' who manages the project as a whole and who is not involved in as a designer or

---

contractor. He provides single-point responsibility for the client and by virtue of his non-involvement in details he is able to concentrate on management.

- It creates a design leader with overall responsibility for the pre-tender design and for sanctioning the contractor's design.

- The contractor's knowledge and experience of the cost implications and buildability of design variables may be utilised to good effect because he contributes to the design.

- It provides financial incentives which encourage contractors to undertake design detailing economical to construct.

- The arrangement by which the contractor undertakes detailed design should reduce 'pre-tender' time and so enable the client to have earlier occupation of the building and an earlier return on his investment. He should incur lower financing costs because of a reduction in the overall project period.

- The system makes provision for the design team and contractor to negotiate upon and alter the pre-tender design before entering into a binding contract. This should reduce variations once the works are in progress.

- There is provision for the design team to name sub-contractors and suppliers who they would require (or prefer) to be invited by the contractor to tender for part of the works. There is no provision for nominated sub-contractors as with the traditional system.

- It supports the use of specifications, rather than bills of quantities, as the basis for obtaining competitive tenders from contractors, despite the preferences of contractors and others for bills of quantities.

- The contractor is required to provide, as a tender document, a priced schedule of activities which supplants bills of quantities and may be used for managing the construction works, monitoring progress, ascertaining the amounts of payments on account to the contractor and negotiating the value of variations.

- Consultants' fees for their services are subject to negotiation rather than being determined by closely defined 'scales' as has been the custom with the traditional system.

- An adjudicator is appointed to decide impartially disputes which may arise in the implementation of the project arrangements. His task is to carry out a prompt investigation and give a decision which is implemented forthwith. There is provision for reference to arbitration 'after the taking over of the works' if the dispute cannot be resolved by the adjudicator.

Form of contract

The ACA form of building contract, BPF edition is available for use with the BPF system.

3. PROJECT TIME: COST RELATIONSHIPS

This publication contains numerous references to the time and cost advantages of various systems for the procurement of buildings.

This section aims to illustrate the extent of the relationship of time to cost.

The report *Faster building for industry*, states that the traditional methods of design and tendering, the various design-and-build options and project management can give good construction times but on average, the use of non-traditional routes tends to produce overall times shorter than those produced by the traditional routes. Figure 8 provides a 'pre-construction timetable' which demonstrates the relative times of the options.

From Figure 8 it may be seen that the use of a negotiated contract enables construction work to commence some seven months earlier than is possible with the 'end-to-end' traditional system. It is reasonable to assume that whichever approach is used for the design, the construction periods will not differ significantly so that the total project period will be reduced if one of the non-traditional or 'fast-track' approaches is used. What effect does this have on the project cost?

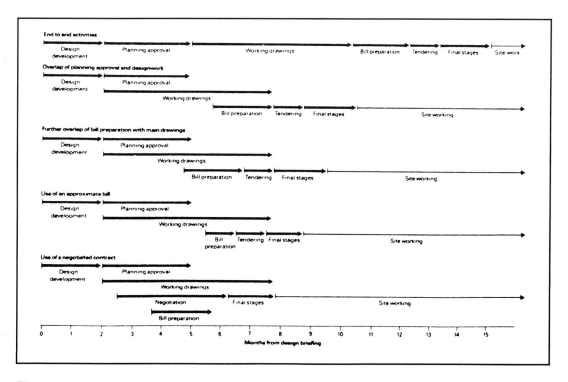

Figure 8 The pre-construction timetable (source, *Faster building for industry*, NEDO, HMSO, 1983)

Case study illustrating the relationship between time and cost

The case study relates to a commercial project in a city centre.

Figure 9 shows alternative expenditure plans for the project assuming use of the traditional system and a 'fast-track' approach.

The data have been provided by a client body specialising in such projects.⑥ Some of the data cannot be more than indicative but the study provides a reasonably reliable basis for cost comparison.

Figure 9(a), the expenditure plan for the traditional system, shows an estimated design period prior to commencement of construction of 12 months. Some design will continue for a period of three months after construction commences. Construction will take 12 months. The total project period is 24 months.

Figure 9(b), the fast-track expenditure plan, shows design and construction periods which are similar to those required for the traditional system. The total project period is 15 months.

The cost of the elements which comprise the project (site, design, construction etc.), are shown in the expenditure plans.

Site acquisition cost (the property itself and associated fees), and design cost are the same for both alternatives.

The construction cost shown in Figure 9(b) is estimated at £½ million more than that required when the traditional system is used. That sum may be regarded as an allowance for the additional cost, (of construction management, accelerated progress, less competitive tendering and similar factors), above that which might be expected if the traditional system were used. Some contractors might question if the cost of construction is, in practice, higher where a fast-track approach is used.

A significant factor in the cost comparison is the timing of expenditure and the associated financing costs. The design team is to be paid as the design is developed. The contractor is to be paid monthly on the basis of the value of work executed. Financing charges follow those payments.

For purposes of the case study an interest rate of 12% pa has been used. Charges have been calculated quarterly.

To demonstrate the advantage of early completion on a commercial project Figure 9(b) shows a rental income for the period between the estimated completion date using a fast-track approach and the estimated completion date using the traditional system, namely, nine months.

	Cost £s K	Months 3	6	9	12	15	18	21	24
Site acquisition	6000	6000 XXXXXX	XXXXXX	XXXXXX	XXXXXX	XXXXXX			
Design	1200	250	250	250	250	200			
Construction	10000					2500 XXXXXX	3000 XXXXXX	3000 XXXXXX	1500 XXXXXX
Quarterly total		6250	250	250	250	2700	3000	3000	1500
Cumulative total		6250	6680	7123	7579	10499	13733	17055	18977
Financing cost (quarterly)		180	193	206	220	234	322	422	524
Total	17200	6430	6873	7329	7799	10733	14055	17477	19501

(a) Expenditure plan – traditional system

	Cost £s K	Months 3	6	9	12	15	18	21	24
Site acquisition	6000	6000 XXXXXX	XXXXXX	XXXXXX	-----	-----			
Design	1200	300	300 XXXXXX	300 XXXXXX	150 XXXXXX	150 XXXXXX			
Construction	10500		3000	3000	3000	1500			
Quarterly total		6300	3300	3300	3150	1650			
Cumulative total		6300	9780	13274	16723	18780			
Financing cost (quarterly)		180	194	299	407	514			
Rental income (£2.3m pa)							(575)	(575)	(575)
Total	17700	6480	9974	13573	17130	19294	18719	18144	17569

(b) Expenditure plan – fast track approach

Figure 9 Time: cost case-study for commercial project

It may be seen that although the construction cost of the fast-track approach is shown as £½ million more than that of the traditional system, at the end of the two year period, when the traditional system would produce a completed building, the fast-track approach shows a saving of £2 million over the traditional system.

In practice, the rent would not be shown as coming back as a saving. A trader developer would sell the development and so accrue a profit, whereas an investment developer would re-negotiate medium term finance, say 25 years, (similar to a mortgage), so that construction finance could be paid off and that from the rent derived he would be able to pay the interest on his medium term finance.

The other benefit to a developer is that by the building being completed sooner it can be valued as a complete development and shown in his accounts as an asset against which he can borrow further money to carry out further developments and grow more quickly.

4. COMPARISON OF PROCUREMENT SYSTEMS

It should be emphasised that the systems as described are subject to great variation.

Client's need

The first component in each of the figures which has been used to illustrate the systems has read: 'client with need for a building' and the following assessments are concerned with that need. The client's viewpoint has been adopted for purposes of the comparison which follows.

Selecting the most appropriate procurement path is largely a matter of determining which performance requirements head the client's list of priorities. These might include:

a) technical complexity;
b) aesthetics/prestige;
c) economy;
d) time;
e) exceptional size or complexity involving input from numerous sources and/or to satisfy several users' requirements;
f) price certainty at an early stage in the project's design development;
g) facility for the client to change/vary the works during the project's construction stage.

In Figure 10 each of the requirements listed above is rated insofar as it is able to satisfy the requirement.

Ratings have been given on a 1 to 5 scale with '1' the minimum and '5' the maximum capacity to meet the requirement. The ratings are the author's assessments of 'satisfaction'. It is assumed that the competence of the personnel involved is similar in all instances – only the systems are being compared. The following comparisons do not take into account all the characteristics of the systems which have been discussed.

Traditional

The traditional system rates '4' for projects with high technical complexity and/or with high aesthetic standards because the design team is not submitted to pressure, provided the design is essentially complete before competitive tenders are sought. In this event the team is able to develop the design rationally. It is the system which has provided the majority of designs in the past.

Competitive tenders ensure that the client obtains the benefit of the lowest building cost. The system should produce a high rating for economy but the rating is reduced because the need to complete the design before commencing construction extends the overall project period. The interest paid by the client on the capital invested during the relatively long project period adds to the total cost of the project.

The sequential nature of the system and the experience gained by a significant number of clients of poor performance on exceptionally large or complex projects has prompted the low ratings for performance requirements (d) and (e).

Price certainty should be capable of achievement provided the project has been fully designed and documented before tenders are sought. Priced bills of quantities facilitate the measurement and valuation of variations during the progress of the works. Hence the high ratings for requirements (f) and (g).

Management system Client's performance requirements/expectations	traditional	management contracting/ construction management	package deal/design-and-build	project manager/client's representative
(a) technical complexity; the project has a high level of structural mechanical services or other complexity.	4	5	4	5
(b) high aesthetic or prestige requirements	5	3	3	4
(c) economy; a commercial or industrial project or project where minimum cost is required.	3	4	4	4
(d) time is of essence; early completion of the project is required.	2	4	5	4
(e) exceptional size and/or administrative complexity; involving varying client's/user requirements, political sensitivity etc.	2	4	4	5
(f) price certainty; is required at an early stage in the project's design development	4	2	4	4
(g) facility for change/variation control by client, users or others during the progress of the works.	5	5	1	4

Figure 10 Rating the systems

Management for a fee

A rating of 5 has been given to requirement (a) because involvement of the construction team at an early stage in the development of the design should facilitate design of complex structures, mechanical services and other elements.

The system would not appear to offer advantages for requirement (b) and a median rating has been given.

Ratings of '4' have been given for performance requirements (c) and (d) because competition between management contractors, initially, and work-package contractors subsequently, produce competition for building works. Because design and construction proceed in parallel the project period is kept to a minimum.

The participation of the management contractor as a member of the 'team', rather than as an outsider makes the system more satisfactory for exceptionally large or complex projects than the traditional system; hence the '4' rating for (e).

Price certainty at an early stage in the project's development is not possible because the cost of building is not known until tenders have been accepted for all work packages. A correspondingly low rating has been given to requirement (f). That said, the client is normally provided with reasonably reliable estimates of the cost of the work packages by the consultant quantity surveyor as the design and construction develops.

A characteristic of these systems is parallel working. This makes it possible to vary the works until the work packages have been placed. Requirement (g) has been given a correspondingly high rating.

The advantages of these systems increase with the size of the project and extent to which time becomes the essence of the contract.

Package deal/design-and-build

Performance requirements (a) and (c) have been given ratings of 4. The involvement of designers with constructors (builders/contractors) on a team basis from the inception stage of the project should produce the expertise to cope with any technical complexity which the project may present. The result should be buildability – an unattractive word describing a necessary characteristic of any construction project which is to succeed. Economy should be achieved because the team is concerned not just with producing a design but with building to a budget. The discipline of designing and building should ensure that materials and components are selected at design stage which are economical and available. These remarks about economy apply also to time. Components or building systems can be designed into the proposed building which will ensure that construction time is kept to a minimum. As the team has both design and construction organisation and control under one roof it can arrange that drawings and specifications are available as and when they are required to ensure that the regular progress of the works is not disrupted. Design and construction progress concurrently not consecutively, which minimises total project time. Ratings of 4 may be less than generous for these performance requirements as may 3 for requirement (b). A rating of 5 has been given to requirement (d).

Package deal systems are used for large and complex projects such as nuclear power plants and petro-chemical developments. For projects of exceptional size or complexity the system should, therefore, be appropriate provided the 'contractor' ensures that a member of the firm who has the managerial expertise is appointed to 'stand outside' the day-to-day activities and hold a balance between design and construction interests. A high, but not the highest, rating has been given to this system in this respect because it is likely that not all firms would have the level of managerial expertise necessary to undertake projects of exceptional size or complexity.

A rating of 4 has been given to requirement (f), price certainty, because the price is normally agreed on the basis of the client's requirements. Provided the requirements are not changed after the contractor has submitted his proposals the price should hold. From this it follows, however, that there is little facility for cost control of changes during the progress of the works. The rating of 1 for requirement (g) reflects this.

Project management/client's representative

Project management developed in response to demands for better management on exceptionally large and complex projects. However, there is increasing evidence that the system is gaining popularity among architects for more run-of-the-mill projects. This departure may at first sight appear surprising because when use of the system increased in the 1960s architects were its principal opponents. They saw their authority being undermined. One can only assume that this change of mind has been made because the experience of some architects on projects which have involved project managers has shown them some advantages of the system.

The term 'client's representative' was adopted by the British Property Federation in 1983 when devising the BPF system in preference to 'project manager'. The system, as such, has not been widely used by clients of the building industry but it is essentially a project manager/client's representative led system and should be regarded as such when making a comparison of procurement systems.

A project manager may be employed with any of the systems described above to the advantage of all. Project management should improve the performance of all the systems because it enables the client, design team and construction team to concentrate its energies and skills on the functions for which they are primarily trained. A project manager should also promote teamwork among designers, builders and installers to the benefit of the client.

However, the greatest advantage should be a clear definition of the client's requirements through a brief to which the project manager is a principal contributor.

For these reasons the system has been rated highly. At the same time, a project manager cannot compensate for 'weaknesses' which are inherent in a system, such as the inability of the package deal system to facilitate cost control of changes during the progress of the works.

Few people would argue with a high rating for project management where exceptional size or complexity are performance requirements.

CONCLUSIONS

When making comparisons it is essential to compare 'like with like'. For this reason it is difficult to make valid comparisons of the alternative systems. Each system has been developed to meet particular client needs. There is no universal system. If one seeks the system which best meets the client's performance requirements in broad terms the ratings discussed above provide a guide for ranking.

To illustrate the method of rating a hypothetical project for a housing association, registered as a charity, which provides homes for the elderly may be used. The Association requires an 'advanced care unit' to meet the needs of residents from its various homes who will undergo treatment as short-stay or out-patients. Operating theatres and specialist equipment will be required. The estimated cost of the unit is between £1m and £1.5m and it will be funded by the sale of investments and from a legacy. Outline planning approval has been given for the unit to be built in the spacious grounds of one of the Association's homes which is listed as a building of architectural interest in a conservation area. An experienced member of the Association's board of management will give his time, freely, to act as client's representative.

Which of the client's performance requirements should be given priority?

The Association requires a building which will satisfy aesthetic standards associated with a listed building and which are consistent with a conservation area (requirement (b)). The Association may also wish to retain the facility to vary the works during their progress as medical technology for the elderly develops (requirement (g)).

The Association owns the site so it will not incur site purchase costs, nor will it incur interest charges on the cash required to purchase the site. Time is not of essence (requirement (d)).

Requirement (e), exceptional size and/or administrative complexity, is not relevant to this project.

The ratings indicate that a traditional approach should be the most appropriate for this project.

5. INCIDENCE OF USE

Background

Reference is made in Section 1 of this publication to the background to change in the procurement of buildings. Until the late 1960s, well after publication of the Emmerson and Banwell reports, the traditional system of procurement was used for the vast majority of building projects. When a client was anxious to 'make a start' on site before the design team had completed the design it was not unusual for the quantity surveyor to take out bills of approximate quantities as a basis for obtaining competitive tenders from contractors. The rates in the bills of quantities being used as the basis for measurement of the works as and when executed.

Project management

About this time, there was discussion at meetings of such as the Joint Building Group[7] where papers with titles such as 'Inter-professional problems in planning and design' were read and there was an acknowledged need for a project manager 'to be leader and to be in full control of the whole operation (this being) of paramount importance'. Such a project manager 'must be able to control the team, completely and co-ordinate the work of the professional experts in it to achieve the maximum efficiency of the collective abilities . . . Above all, he must bear in mind the economic and technical aspects of the problems'. The author took it for granted that an architect or engineer would be the project manager.

In 1966, Brett-Jones[8], suggested that 'the first act in the management of any project is taken not by the client's decision to build but his decision to call someone to advise him as to whether he should build or not and how he should go about it'. Brett-Jones predicted the appointment of 'a project manager drawn from any of the professions for schemes of size'. Clearly, the project manager was not an established role but it was not unknown.

In 1974 the RICS made a study of quantity surveying practice[9] which suggested that approximately 4% of the private quantity surveying practices studied undertook project management regularly and approximately 20% spasmodically. There is, however, reason to believe that some surveyors studied may have interpreted the term project management as relating to management for contractors rather than for clients. The figures quoted above should therefore be regarded with some caution. Nevertheless, project management was established if not widely used during the first half of the 1970s.

In 1975 the Presidents of both the Institute of Quantity Surveyors and the RICS were advising their members to equip themselves to take on new roles including that of project manager.[10]

1975 saw the NEDO publication *The public client and the construction industry* which, incidentally, suggested that on some projects there was reason to employ a project manager[11] and the CIOB arranged a conference in conjunction with the PSA which reviewed the state of the project management art. [12]

In the absence of significant published statistical data concerned with the incidence of use of the various procurement systems until 1983 it is not possible to determine the extent of the impact of the project manager on the construction industry's performance. The interest in the subject may, however, give some guide to the impact and to ascertain the extent of interest. Figure 11 plots the number of publications issued each year on procurement systems during the period 1967 to 1988. It is apparent that there were very few publications until 1975 from which year the interest in the subject was sustained. Interest appears to have been at its peak in 1977.

The first study which provides significant statistical evidence of the incidence of use, albeit for only a specialised sector of the industry, is the NEDO report *Faster building for industry*[13] published in 1983 which reviews the state of the art in that sector in 1982.

The report studied 56 industrial projects and recommended that the client ensured that someone acted as the focal point for his interests, either in-house or from outside and found that 9% of the projects employed such a person.

NEDO's subsequent report for commerce[14] in 1986 repeated and strengthened the recommendation given in 1982. 48% of the commercial projects employed project managers. Many of the clients for these projects were developers who had their own in-house project managers or had well established relationships with consultant project managers.

The clients of the projects studied by both the NEDO reports should, however, be regarded generally as informed and experienced clients, as it were, the 'professional' clients of the construction industry. It is an irony that the clients with most experience of the construction industry tend to employ project managers to a greater extent than the 'occasional' client. It is, therefore, unlikely that project managers are employed across the industry generally on as high a percentage of projects as those stated in the NEDO reports.

There is, then, a general recognition that there is a need for a client to appoint a representative to act on his behalf in the dialogue between the client's organisation and the team appointed to procure the building. Without the support of statistical evidence it is not possible to state the incidence of use of project managers at the close of the 1980s but it is probably reasonable to suggest that for a very significant number of building projects in excess of, say £3 million in value, a project manager is employed but that a project manager is not employed on the majority of smaller projects.

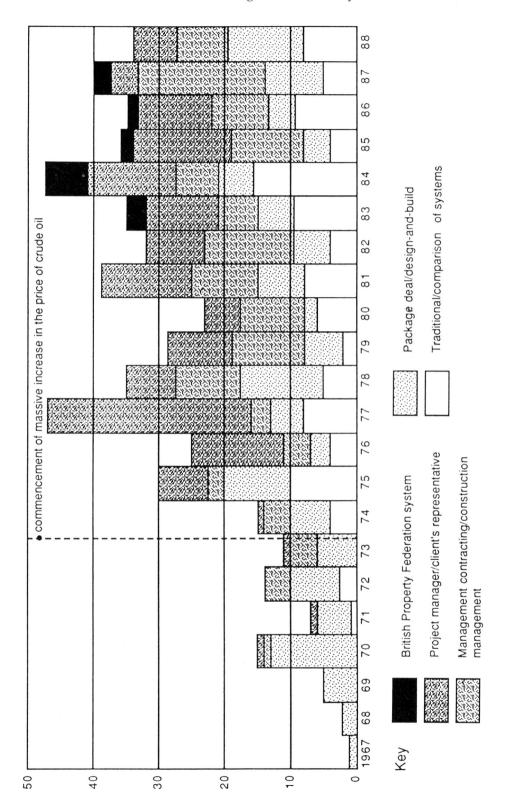

Figure 11 An indication of interest in alternative systems (derived from the number of published papers concerned with alternative systems: year of publication which comprise the bibliography)

Management contracting/construction management

Bovis has operated management contract/fee approaches to building procurement for more than 60 years. In the second half of the 1980s the group extended its activities to construction management. Apart from Bovis few firms took management contracting seriously until after the 1973 international oil crisis. Figure 11 shows that the construction industry and its clients' interest increased significantly in 1978 when the effect of high interest and high inflation rates had been experienced, particularly, by the industry's clients.

The NEDO report on faster building for industry indicates that in the industrial sector in 1982 14% of the 56 projects studied were carried out by management contractors. The NEDO report on faster building for commerce indicates that in 1986 9% of the projects were carried out by management contracting firms. The report states that the management contracts had 'a lower success rate' in achieving early completion than other 'non-traditional projects' but generally the non-traditional projects were completed faster than traditional projects.

The most significant surveys of procurement systems which offer an opportunity to study trends in the incidence of use have been made by the Junior Organisation, Quantity Surveyors Division of the RICS.[15] Figures 12, 13, 14, 15 and 16 have been derived from these surveys.

Figure 12 shows that management contracting firms carried out 12% of the total value of building work in 1984 which value increased to almost 15% in 1985 and decreased to 9.5% in 1987.

Figure 13 shows estimates of the number of projects carried out using management contracts or construction management systems during the years 1984, 1985 and 1987.

Figure 14 has been prepared from the data in Figure 13. Figure 14(a), which represent projects with a value not exceeding £0.5 million, shows a massive decrease in numbers during the period 1984 to 1987. More remarkable than the decrease is the fact that so many projects of less than £0.5 million were, in 1984 and 1985, carried out using management contracts.

Figure 14(b) to 14(e) suggest that for larger projects management contracts appear to have held their own. This supports the opinion of marketing personnel in major management contracting firms in 1989. There is reason to believe that many of the smaller, more recently founded firms, frequently as divisions of major contracting firms, may experience a reduction in their work loads during the closing decade of the 20th century.[16]

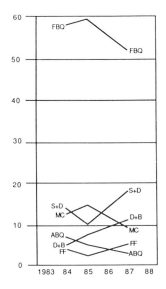

Figure 12   Alternative methods of procurement (percentage by value of work)

Key to procurement methods used:

ABQ   lump sum – approximate bills of quantities
D&B   design-and-build
FBQ   lump sum – firm bills of quantities
FF   prime cost sum plus fixed fee
MC   management contract
S&D   lump sum – specification and drawings

Year	Contract size in £m/# of contracts					
	<£0.5	£0.5–£1	£1–3	£3–10	£10+	total
1984	350	50	125	63	50	638
1985	200	67	126	111	44	548
1987	69	28	110	97	48	352

Figure 13   Management contracts (by size and number)

Package deal/design-and-build

Figure 11 indicates that from 1967, interest in the package deal/design-and-build approach was steadily maintained and significantly increased in 1987 and 1988.

Established in 1957, IDC claims to be the pioneer of modern design-and-build techniques and with a turnover in excess of £70 million in 1988, the largest. IDC is to design-and-build as Bovis is to management fee contracting.

5. Incidence of Use

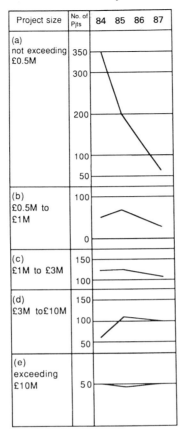

Figure 14 Management contracts by size number.

In recent years there has been a massive increase in the number of firms offering design-and-build services. Contract Journal's survey in March 1989[17] suggests that the market has grown at a rate of between 15% to 20% per annum over the last five years. All the firms' forecasts are of continued growth at the same or a faster rate during the period 1990 to 1995.

The NEDO report on faster building for industry indicates that in the industrial building sector in 1982, 34% of the 56 projects were carried out by design-and-build firms.

The NEDO report on faster building for commerce indicates that in the commercial building sector in 1986, 16% of the projects were carried out by design-and-build firms.

The earlier NEDO report, which quotes 34% for industrial building, is not far removed from the figure estimated by Len Whitting, IDC group chief executive, who suggests that design-and-build contractors carried out £2 billion of the £6.4

billion, (30%), of the total workload handled by contractors in the industrial and commercial sectors in 1988.[17]

Figure 2 shows that design-and-build firms carried out 5% of work (by value) in 1984 which increased to 8% in 1985 and to 12% in 1987.

On the basis of the trend shown in Figure 13 some 50% of all building work, by value of work carried out annually, could be carried out by design-and-build contractors by the end of the century.

Figure 15 shows estimates of the number of projects carried out using design-and-build contracts during the years 1984, 1985 and 1987.

Figure 16 suggests that design-and-build contracts are being less used for projects smaller than £0.5 million but for the larger projects (represented by Figure 16(b) to (e)) there has been a marked increase. The most pronounced increase has been in projects in the £1 million to £3 million range, (figure 14(c)). It may be inferred from figure 16(c) that the design-and-build approach has established a significant hold on medium-sized projects.

Year	Contract size in £m/# of contracts					
	<£0.5	£0.5–£1	£1–3	£3–10	£10+	total
1984	544	169	106	38	0	857
1985	569	251	207	104	17	1148
1987	311	255	311	117	35	1029

Figure 15   Design-and-build by contract size and number

Europe and 1992

With 1992 and the prospect of a single market approaching, the building industry in Britain looks to the continent of Europe as a potential source of work and vice versa.

To what extent are the contractual arrangements discussed consistent with those on the continent?

Numerous observers from Britain have visited Europe to investigate aspects of building procurement in one or more countries. Their findings vary considerably depending on the opinions of the persons or organisations with whom they communicated. Participants in the construction industries in other countries are as subjective in their responses as their counterparts in the UK.

5. Incidence of Use

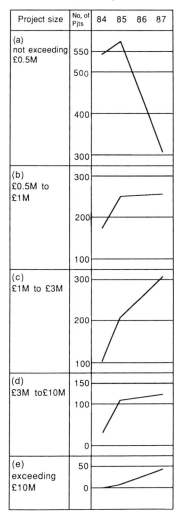

Figure 16 Design-and-build by contract size and number.

The following review draws on published texts, personal communications with observers and field studies over a period of years. It provides only an introduction to the procurement processes in France, West Germany and Sweden.

France

The first stage design, during which the client's needs are expressed as a 'grand conception', is traditionally the province of the Ecoles des Beaux Arts educated architect.

The development of the design is carried out by engineers, technicians and administrative personnel in bureaux d'etudes, technical offices, which perform the functions undertaken by the various consultant engineers, quantity surveyors etc in the UK. The bureaux' activities may include town planning, cost benefit analyses and management and supervision of projects. Their activities include project cost control.

The construction manager operates under the title 'maitre d'oeuvre' (master of works).

Comparable with the project manager's role is that of the promoteur who most frequently plays a part in major commercial developments but is not unknown in other sectors of the French construction industry's activities.

Construction firms are similar to those in Britain in that they vary greatly in size and capability. Contracts for projects may be between client and a main contractor or between client and several specialist contractors. The latter, 'lots séparés', arrangement is more generally used.

In recent years there has been a significant increase in the use of design-and-build.

Contractual arrangements in Belgium and Spain are probably nearer to those in France than to other European countries but Spain appears to be interested in British contractual arrangements.

West Germany

All stages of design are undertaken by the architect/engineer who may be university or technical institute educated or, exceptionally, self taught.

Construction works for the majority of projects are carried out by specialist contractors each of whom has a contract with the client.

Construction management may be undertaken by specialist staff within the architect's office or by an independent construction manager or 'bauleiter', who is responsible for production and cost management. His tasks include preparation of the equivalent of bills of quantities as a tool for cost management.

An alternative course is for the architect to appoint a management contractor, (bauträger) to co-ordinate site activity.

In recent years the 'traditional' (British) contractual arrangement has gained ground. Reports vary as to the incidence of use of the various contractual arrangements. Main contractors are by no means unknown and probably increasing in number.

Contractors frequently undertake design-and-build contracts for which works they employ architects to design, usually on an ad hoc basis.

Other contractual arrangements include the formation of ad hoc consortia and joint ventures. This is a common approach for major projects.

Independent project managers may act in much the same manner as in the UK.

Contractual arrangements in the Netherlands and in Switzerland are probably nearer to those in West Germany than to other countries in Europe.

Sweden

Sweden pioneered the concept of the project manager, (byggleder), appointed by the client to head and co-ordinate the building team and act as a single line of communication with the client. Many project management firms are well established and offer comprehensive services worldwide.

Architects and/or engineers undertake the design of buildings and all structural and engineering services. The role of the byggandskontrolant approximates to that of construction manager or, perhaps, quantity surveyor. The role of the kalkylator is also similar to that of the quantity surveyor but the kalkylator's role is not as sophisticated as that of his British counterpart. Specialist contractors entering into separate 'works contracts' with the client predominate but traditional (British) contracts are used regularly.

The other Scandinavian countries have similar contractual arrangements to those in Sweden but their markets are not as large and their industries are not as developed.

Italy is regarded as having more in common with British procurement arrangements than with other European countries.

The overall scene in the European Community

To some extent the approaches by the countries referred to above appear to mirror national traits. The French with a bias, (in British eyes), to elitism and social class distinctions tend to separate the 'art' from the 'craft'.

The German tendency to relish technical expertise leads to stratified professional 'classes' with varying levels of social recognition.

The Swedish lead in human resource management has led to Scandinavia recognising the need to have building projects 'professionally' managed rather than managed by designers who had little or no training in management skills.

There is, then, a rag-bag of alternative systems for building procurement operating in Europe with most, if not all, of which the British industry is familiar. There is ample evidence that in property development the United Kingdom is probably ahead of other countries in Europe. British property development firms are established in many major cities in Europe.

There is considerable evidence that there is little by way of standard procedures for the procurement of buildings in any of the countries and certainly there is no procedure that may be regarded as a standard in Europe.

Summary

This section has concentrated on the alternatives rather than the traditional system but this does not mean that the alternatives have supplanted the traditional.

NEDO surveys for the reports on building for industry and commerce found that in 1982, 43% of the industrial projects and in 1986, 70% of the commercial projects were carried out using traditional arrangements.

Figure 12 shows that projects using firm bills of quantities stood at 58% in 1984, increased to 59% in 1984 but decreased to 52% in 1987.

In addition to the projects using 'firm' bills of quantities were the projects using approximate bills of quantities and those using specifications and drawings because both these categories almost certainly adopted, what might be termed, 'new traditional' contracts. During 1984 to 1987 the use of approximate bills decreased from 6½% to 3%, which was more than offset by the increase in the use of specifications and drawings from 13½% to 18%.

The editor of the RICS JO (QS) surveys states that they probably understate the increasing importance of design-and-build contracting. The 'fixed fee' contracts were almost certainly carried out using in-house or consultant construction managers. As this contractual arrangement represents, at most, 5% of the value of work, its significance is not great.

Only passing reference has been made to the use of the BPF system. The contribution of this system to the industry's attitudes and approaches to building procurement is acknowledged but in May 1989 the incidence of use was unknown[18]. Statistically, its contribution is almost certainly insignificant.

The position at the close of the 1980s is that the incidence of use of management contracts is decreasing and design-and-build contracts is increasing at a rate which could lead to a point where 50% of the value of work is, by the end of the century, carried out using design-and-build contracts. Changing attitudes among clients, designers and builders appear to favour its growth.

6. CLIENTS' NEEDS AND EXPECTATIONS

Survey of clients' needs and expectations

Clients of the construction industry range from those who commission building works once or twice in their lifetimes and do not know what to expect to those who are, in effect, 'professional' clients with regular projects, clearly defined needs and high expectations.

To ascertain the nature of these needs and expectations a survey of 50 clients was carried out during October and November 1989.

The clients in the sample have been grouped as follows:

Group A

'Occasional' clients who build for their own use or occupation such as church authorities, public service utilities, industrialists, manufacturers, commercial undertakings, medical practitioners etc. etc. (52% of the sample).

Group B

Those acquiring land and/or property and developing them to let on their own behalf or to sell to pension funds or similar investors. These are referred to below as the developers (18% of the sample).

Group C

Housing associations; both local authority backed and private. The group includes associations providing homes for the elderly (8% of the sample).

Group D

Local authorities at district and county level (10% of the sample).

Group E

Health care bodies; National Health Service and private sector (12% of the sample).

Views were obtained from two members of staff of the Property Services Agency and these are included in the text. The PSA has not been included in the statistical analysis.

The survey provides a sample of client types with a disproportionate emphasis on clients who had commissioned more than ten projects in the past ten years and on clients undertaking larger projects. Nevertheless, it provides some indication of clients' needs and expectations.

Client contact with building team

The questionnaire separates those persons who are employed full-time by the client as project managers and those who are engaged as consultant project managers.

Taken as a whole, 54% of the clients have within their own organisations a person (or persons) who acts as the focal point through which the corporate requirements pass to the building team. Such a person most frequently holds the title project manager, project co-ordinator or similar. The title 'clients' representative' seldom occurs.

An analysis of the sample shows the point of contact between clients and the building teams in the various client groups to be as shown in Figure 17.

	In-house project manager %	Consultant project manager %	Architect %
Group A	60	8	32
Group B	98	2	–
Group C	25	–	75
Group D	–	–	100
Group E	50	–	50

Figure 17   Client contact with building team

Figure 17 shows that 60% of the Group A, 'occasional', clients employ in-house project managers but this may be a misleading statistic because a disproportionate number of the clients in the sample are major commercial firms and public service bodies. A sample containing smaller projects for clients who commissioned building works infrequently would almost certainly show greater employment of an architect as the leader of the team. With only one or two exceptions clients who commission building works infrequently and whose works are typically less than £3 million for each project, tend to employ an architect to design and manage the works in the traditional manner.

All but one of the developers, (Group B), employ in-house project managers; a major firm of project managers provides management services for the client who does not.

The samples in Groups C, D and E are too small to be statistically representative but they are believed to give a reliable indication of the contact between client and the building team. Housing associations and local authorities tend to employ architects either in-house or as consultants to act in the traditional manner.

Health authorities projects tend to be larger and more complex and project managers are more in evidence.

The majority of clients, approximately 80% of the sample, decide on the contractual arrangement, often in consultation with the construction team.

Clients for smaller projects tend to rely on the architect and quantity surveyor to decide on the contractual arrangements to be used for procurement of their works.

Client involvement

The majority of clients in the sample expect to be involved in the project during both the design and construction stages of the project's life.

Figure 18 shows, as a percentage of each client group, the extent to which the clients in the sample expect to be involved in running the project.

	Group	A %	B %	C %	D %	E %
* only at initial design stage		8	–	25	40	17
* during the whole of the design stage		4	–	–	20	–
* during both design and construction stages		88	100	75	40	83

Figure 18 Client involvement in the project

Contractual arrangements

Figure 19 shows, as a percentage of each client group, the extent to which clients have used various contractual arrangements during the ten year period up to the survey.

Developers, Group B, show the greatest propensity to use alternative contractual arrangements, local authorities the least. Considered as a whole, 100% of clients have used the traditional, 56% project management, 46% management contracting, 22% construction management, 56% design-and-build and 4% the British Property Federation system.

Local authority clients refer to their councils' standing orders as a reason why they tend to make little use of alternative contractual arrangements. The Property Services Agency has no such inhibitions and uses whichever arrangement is considered appropriate for the project under consideration.

Group	A	B	C	D	E
Traditional	100	100	100	100	100
Project manager	59	100	33	20	50
Management contracting	50	100	–	–	33
Construction management	27	38	–	–	17
Design-and-build	59	75	33	20	83
British Property Federation system	–	13	–	–	–

Figure 19   Use of contractual arrangements

For future projects, the majority of clients do not anticipate using different contractual arrangements but most do not have closed minds.

Several Group A clients, 18%, are considering using design-and-build and one *more* management contracts. One is considering using the British Property Federation system and another is developing its own form of contract.

The majority of developer clients, Group B, are already using most of the arrangements but 22% of the sample are considering design-and-build, 11% the British Property Federation system and 11% construction management. The last mentioned arrangement for exceptionally large projects.

42% of the housing associations, local authorities and health authorities are considering the use of design-and-build.

Clients' priorities

The questionnaire suggests technical complexity, aesthetics/prestige, economy, time of essence, exceptional size, price certainty at an early stage and facility for variations as a list of *priorities* from which clients might select three which are the most relevant to their projects. Figure 20 shows their priorities. The numbers are rounded percentages of the number of clients in the sample.

During interviews some clients remarked that the list of priorities made no provision for 'low maintenance cost/quality'. Some remarked that 'value for money' is their top priority. Value for money is considered to be insufficiently specific to be recorded as a priority but a record was made of low maintenance cost/quality when this was suggested as a priority. Provision has not been made in the figure for this priority because it was not suggested to all who took part in the survey. There is no doubt that a significant number of clients regard low maintenance cost as a priority for their projects.

Columns 1 to 7 in the figure are self-evident. The numbers in column 8 are the sums of those to their left and those in column 9 are the order of rank for first, second and third priorities. The numbers in column 10 are the sum of those in column 8 and those in column 11 are the order of rank for the priorities listed in column 1.

Figure 20 shows that *economy* and *time* are the priorities of most clients. Economy is marginally of more importance as first priority. Price certainty at an early stage in the development of the project's design is the next most important priority followed by appearance (aesthetics/prestige). Several clients remarked that their priorities varied from project to project.

1	2	3	4	5	6	7	8	9	10	11
				Groups						
Priority	Ranking	A	B	C	D	E	Total	Ranking	Total	Ranking
Technical complexity	1	–	–	–	–	4	4	4		
	2	6	–	–	–	–	6	5		
	3	2	–	–	–	2	4	6	14	6
Aesthetics/ prestige	1	12	10	–	–	–	22	2		
	2	4	2	–	–	2	8	4		
	3	10	–	2	2	–	14	=3	44	4
Economy	1	12	4	2	2	4	24	1		
	2	10	4	2	6	4	26	1		
	3	6	4	2	2	–	14	=3	64	=1
Time of essence	1	12	4	–	–	2	18	4		
	2	10	6	2	2	–	20	2		
	3	14	4	2	4	2	26	1	64	=1
Price certainty	1	10	–	2	6	2	20	3		
	2	12	–	2	–	4	18	3		
	3	12	4	–	–	2	18	2	56	3
Facility for variations	1	–	–	–	–	–	–	=6		
	2	4	–	–	–	–	4	6		
	3	4	4	–	–	4	12	5	16	5
Exceptional size	1	–	–	–	–	–	–	=6		
	2	–	–	–	–	–	–	7		
	3	2	–	–	–	–	2	7	2	7

Figure 20 Clients' priorities

Clients' observations on project organisation

80% of the clients in the sample believe that the organisation of their projects could or should be better.

Their comments are discussed below under seven headings. The comments which occurred most frequently are discussed first.

Architectural design and co-ordination

The most numerous comments, (35%), are concerned with the architect's performance. The principal complaint is concerned with the architect's inability to design within pre-determined cost limits and, in one instance, failure to follow his brief. One client suggests alternative designs should have been provided for his consideration.

Most clients regard the architect as the design leader and criticise the lack of teamwork between members of the design team. These failures are attributed to lack of professional experience and insufficient staff being provided by the consultants. A 'better understanding of the client's needs by the architect' is required.

Problems did not end with completion of the design stage. Indeed, lack of co-ordination and control of the works is a frequent cause of complaint. Complaining about this aspect, a client with experience of only one project comments about her architect that he was; 'a great designer but lacking in management skills'. A 'regular' client points out that the designer is the essential link in the project and when he fails it is a serious matter. Another, that some architects fail at the commencement of the project to provide adequate information to the contractor and that there is a 'lack of mechanical and engineering co-ordination into designs'. The complaint about lack of control extends to control of costs.

A client who has built more than ten times during the previous 10 years and whose building works are in the £0.5 to £1 million price range has employed both architects and project managers as point of contact. He states that the organisation has been better on the projects managed by project managers.

Another small, infrequent client of the building industry who is in the minority of those who considers the organisation of his projects could not be better, uses the services of a project manager when he has cause to build.

Communication and liaison

The next most frequent cause of comment, (25%), is poor communication. As one client puts it, 'between all members of the team at all stages and in all forms of communication, written, oral etc'.

Another client with previous experience in the petro-chemical industries compares his present experience unfavourably with those industries. In the building industry; 'there is a lack of liaison between members of the team and lack of feedback'.

One client actually uses the words of the 1962 Emmerson Report with reference to the divorce of design from production being the cause of so many of the building industry's problems.

Positive steps to improve communication are being taken by a developer client with considerable experience of using the British Property Federation system. The company is constantly refining its contractual arrangements with the aim of 'enforcing marriage between architect, structural engineer and contractor'. The 'refinement' moves more quickly when the building industry's work-load is light and members of the team are concerned with keeping full orderbooks.

Client failures

25% of the clients in the sample are critical of their own performance. In some instances positive steps have been taken to put their houses in order.

Perceived weaknesses are poor briefing and a tendency to commence site works before the design has been sufficiently developed. As one client puts it; 'more haste, less speed'. Another remarks that a certain project could have been less costly but building economy had been sacrificed for early completion.

The principal problem experienced by clients when they 'inflict their own wounds' is their failure to define their requirements in order to obviate variations at a later date. Lack of co-operation within the client body, particularly in the larger organisation, may lead to the project manager being unable to act effectively as the focal point between corporate requirements and the building team which will realise them.

Contractors

10% of the clients in the sample criticise contractors. One criticism is that contractors fail to co-ordinate sub-contractors' works. Their failure to complete the works in the contract period may lead to the client deducting liquidated damages. To the credit of contractors, a major industrialist is highly critical of his consultants but comments that he is 'rarely let down by contractors'.

Claims and delays

The words 'delay' and 'claim' occur in 8% of the clients' comments. Where the delays lead to successful application of the liquidated damages clause by the client the contractor must be regarded as being at fault and reference has been made to such situations above.

Other delays, which lead to successful claims by the contractor, are caused by various factors some of which, such as poor communications, have also been referred to above. A housing association client remarks that highly competitive tenders lead to 'claims and over-runs'. Claims appear to occur more frequently on traditional contracts.

Engineering services

Reference has been made above to the failure of the design team to satisfactorily incorporate services engineering installations into the design and to the failure of contractors to manage the sub-contractors concerned. The complexity and magnitude of engineering services, particularly on some major projects, is referred to by clients when discussing ways in which the organisation of their projects have proved unsatisfactory.

Human factors

Indirect reference has been made above to the human factor when considering communication failures and lack of teamwork. More than 30% of the clients comment on those aspects. In addition, other clients make particular reference to the extent to which 'people' are the 'variable factor' which determines the success or failure of their projects.

The short note of an interview with a major developer client encapsulates the views of many when it refers to the need for; 'better co-ordination of information in the team and better communication. Good people are the key'.

Summary

Not surprisingly the needs of clients in terms of contractual organisation vary widely. The more experienced and knowledgeable the client, the more he tends to identify a single point of contact, a person to act as his representative and leave that person to manage the project. For most clients that person is not an architect. The first-time client for one of the smallest projects referred to her architect as 'a great designer but lacking in management skills'. One of the largest and most sophisticated property owners in Britain even referred enquiries in connection with the survey to the company's consultant project managers.

Increasingly, clients look to a manager rather than an architect to manage their projects. This applies to large clients such as the PSA, to developers and to many of the occasional clients with some experience of building. The exceptions are local authorities and, to a lesser extent, housing associations which are bound by 'standing orders'.

The majority of clients expect to be involved in running the project during both the design and construction stages. The extent to which they are involved because work on site is frequently commenced before the design is completed, is difficult to ascertain. Whatever the reason for their involvement, many clients' experience leads them to expect involvement at both design and construction stages. They may not wish to have involvement over such a long period but they expect it.

7. REFERENCES

1 (1962) Survey of problems before the construction industries report prepared for the Minister of Works by Sir Harold Emmerson. HMSO.
2 (1964) The planning and management of contracts for building and civil engineering works. Report of the (Banwell) Committee. HMSO.
3 NEDO. (1975) The public client and the construction industries. HMSO.
4 NEDO. (1985) Thinking about building. HMSO.
5 NEDO. (1988) Faster building for commerce. NEDO.
6 VICKERY, J. Greycoat Group: personal communication.
7 VINEY, T.L. (1965) paper at meeting of the Joint Building Group of the ICE, January. Reported in *The Builder* 2 April.
8 BRETT-JONES, A.T. (1966) Project management *Chartered Surveyor*, January.
9 RICS. (1974) Practice of quantity surveying.
10 FRANKS, J. (1975) Presidential address to IQS, *Quantity Surveyor*, August, Doig, D., presidential address to RICS, *Chartered Surveyor*, November.
11 NEDO. (1975) Ibid.
12 IOB/PSA. (1975) Conference, Getting buildings designed and built. London. April
13 NEDO. (1983) Faster building for industry. HMSO.
14 NEDO. (1988) Ibid.
15 The Junior Organisation, Quantity Surveyors Division, RICS published reports of surveys into forms of contract, preferences and usage in *Chartered Quantity Surveyor*, January 1986, December 1986 and January 1989. The data contained in figures 13, 14, 15, 16 and 17 are derived from the reports. Figure 13 is derived from Table 5 in the reports. The 'numbers of contracts' shown in Figure 14 and 16 have been obtained by adjusting the numbers shown in Table 5 by the 'capture' percentages stated in the reports. It is appreciated that such extrapolations are subject to error but the resultant numbers should be sufficiently accurate to provide a valid indication of trends. The author gratefully acknowledges the source of the data. Any errors in interpretation are his own.
16 FRANKS J., (1989) Survey of ten design-and-build firms concerned with market trends and tendering procedures. July.
17 (1989) Design-and-build. *Contract Journal*, 30 July.
18 DENNY R., (1989) Personal communication. May.

8. BIBLIOGRAPHY

The following annotated bibliography is in chronological order with the most recent items coming first. It is based on material first published in the CIOB bi-monthly publication *Building Management Abstracts* from 1970 onwards.

1989

571
RICS
PROJECT MANAGEMENT AGREEMENT AND CONDITIONS OF ENGAGEMENT
1989. pp 12

570
RICS
PROJECT MANAGEMENT AGREEMENT AND CONDITIONS OF ENGAGEMENT. GUIDANCE NOTE.
1989. pp 8

569
A. Griffith
DESIGN-BUILD PROCUREMENT AND BUILDABILITY
CIOB Technical Information Service Paper No. 112, 1989, pp 8
The design-build method of procurement is considered in the context in the industry's increasing expectation of innovative and improved method. Potential benefits and problems of application are considered and the likely implications for clients, contractors and the professions are addressed.

568
B. Dodworth
DESIGN AND BUILD
Contracts Management 1989 November, pp 19–20
The advantages of design and build are summarised.

567
R. M. Denny
BUILDING AND CONTRACT MANAGEMENT
Contracts Management 1989 November, pp 15–18
The BPF system of procurement is described.

566
R. Fellows
RISK IN MANAGEMENT CONTRACTING
Chartered Builder 1989 *1* November/December, pp 32–34

565
M. Evamy
ST OLAF REVIVED BY WALLIS
Contract Journal 1989 *350* August 17, pp 10–11
It is claimed that use of BPF contract on a refurbishment job made a significant contribution to its success.

564
PROJECT MANAGEMENT
Chartered Surveyor Weekly 1989 August 17, pp 27–29, 31–33, 35–36. A series of articles is presented covering basic reviews as seen through they eyes of PMI; liability of the project manager, PM courses; an agreement between PM and client formed by the RICS; case studies on recent jobs and some of the key personalities.

563
J. S. Russell
CONTRACTOR PRE QUALIFICATION DATA FOR CON-STRUCTION MANAGERS
CM Advisor 1989 *7* July, pp 6–7
The results are summarised of a survey of the impact various factors have on construction managers decision making process regarding contractor pre-qualification.

562
P. Harris
MANAGEMENT CONTRACTING: AN INSIDER'S VIEW
Architect, Builder, Contractor & Developer 1989 March, pp 24, 26–27
An interview with John McKenna, MC of Taylor Woodrow management contracting concerning developments in the way of the contractural arrangement is operated.

561
DESIGN AND BUILD SURVEY
Contract Journal 1989 *348* March 2, pp 24–26, 28–30, 32, 34–37
The survey is based on the responses of 56 contractors, identifies under each organisation the level of design build activity, its financial contribution and recent clients.

560
J. Gosney
RISE AND RISE OF DESIGN AND BUILD
Contract Journal 1989 *348* March 2, pp 18–20
The increasing rise is discussed of design build, the views of a number of practitioners being included to demonstrate the basis of its success.

559
P. Harris
MANAGEMENT CONTRACTING: AN INSIDER'S VIEW A B C & D 1989 March, pp 22–24, 26–27
An interview with John McKennan, MD of Taylor Woodrow Management Contracting on the way the system of procurement is operated within the firm.

1988

558

Dearle & Henderson

MANAGEMENT CONTRACTING: A PRACTISE MANUAL

1988. Spon. pp 113

A text for quantity surveyors which deals in turn with management contracting and the QS; selection procedures and documentation; and financial management. Appendices provide sample contracts, forms and documents.

557

CIOB

PROJECT MANAGEMENT IN BUILDING

1988 3rd Edition pp 32

Project management as practised in both the UK and abroad is examined before the objectives of project management and the role and duties of the project manager are described. The second part deals with education for project management, a framework being provided against which the syllabus of any individual course may be compared.

556

CIOB

CODE OF ESTIMATING PRACTICE: SUPPLEMENT 2. DESIGN AND BUILD

1988. pp 40

555

S. Hornby

FINANCE REQUIRED FOR WORKING CAPITAL IN MANAGEMENT CONTRACTING

RICS Occasional Paper. 1988. p16

A comparison is made of the financing of ten firms providing management contracting with ten general contractors. It is shown that less finance is required for management contacting but that there are significantly lower profit margins. Returns on capital employed were found to be similar.

554

D. Hobson

MANAGEMENT CONTRACTING – A STEP IN THE RIGHT DIRECTION?

RICS Occasional Paper 1988. 2nd edition. p25

In addition to providing an overview, consideration is given to the role the QS can play.

553

H. Dawson

DESIGN AND BUILD. A CLIENTS VIEWPOINT

Chartered Quantity Surveyor 1988 *11* November, pp 29–30

552

P. Graham

MANAGEMENT CONTRACTS. DREAM OF FEES

Chartered Quantity Surveyor 1988 *11* October, pp 24/25

Fee levels for Quantity Surveyors working on management contracts are discussed.

551

I. Davies

INDUSTRIAL AND COMMERCIAL BUILDING

Building Techology & Management 1988 *26* August/September, p20

The approach is described of IDC to in-house design and project management, without or with construction management.

550

M. Barnes

PROJECT MANAGEMENT TODAY IV. ORGANISING TO ACHIEVE

Civil Engineering Surveyor 1988 *13* May, pp 23–25

The responsibilities of the project manager are identified before consideration is given to various forms of procurement including target cost, cost reimbursable, design and build and management contracting.

549

Gardiner & Theobald

CHOOSING A FAST TRACK PRESCRIPTION

Building 1988 *253* April 29, p 30

Some of the major limitations of management contracting are discussed. Of particular note is the increased reluctance of trade contractors to accept the additional risks without consequent enhanced financial rewards and the trend toward 'double prelims'.

548

M. Bar-Hillel

SWEET SUCCESS WITH TARGET COST

CS Weekly 1988 April 21, p25

A design and building variant – target cost – as developed by Cyril Sweet & Partners is outlined.

547

R. M. Skitmore and D. E. Marsden

WHICH PROCUREMENT SYSTEM? TOWARDS A UNIVERSAL PROCUREMENT SELECTION TECHNIQUE

Construction Management & Economics 1988 *6* Spring, pp 71-89

Two approaches are described which aid the selection of the most appropriate procurement arrangements. The first is a multi-attribute technique based on the NEDO procurement path decision chart and the other approach is by means of discriminate analysis.

546

PROJECT CASE BOOK: RAF BRAMPTON

Contract Journal 1988 March 31, pp 12–14

The construction of headquarters buildings for RAF Support Command HQ is described. Management by Conder on a design and build basis, the fast track approach adopted allowed completion within 21 months. Particular attention is given to the design challenge, procurement, planning and running the job.

545

S. Marshal and R. Morledge

RISKING DESIGN & BUILD

Chartered Quantity Surveyor 1988 *10* March pp 25–26

The risk elements associated with design and build are discussed with reference to *Bolam v Friern Hospital Management Committee* and *Greaves v Baynham Meikle & Partners*.

544
M. Spring
HEALTHY RUSH OF BLOOD
Building 1988 *253* March 18, pp 43-47
The construction is described of the N. London Blood Transfusion Centre which was a fast track management contract based on flexible layouts and prefabricated components.

543
K. Stansfield
MANAGEMENT CONTRACTING ON MAJOR PUBLIC SECTOR PROJECTS
Construction 1988 (63) February, pp 29–30
Taylor Woodrow's approach to management contracting is described.

542
F. H. Archer & D. W. M. Knight
HONG KONG & SHANGHAI BANKING CORPORATION HEADQUARTERS CONSTRUCTION
ICE Proceedings. 1988 *84* Part 1. February, pp 43–65
An outline is given of the construction sequence with particular reference to the constraints imposed, the problems encountered and the solutions devised to complete on schedule, a fast track, high-quality project. Examples are given of the proven flexibility of management contracting. New construction methods and materials are described, together with the adoption of traditional temporary works.

541
P. Reina
DESIGN & BUILD TAKES SHELTER
Contract Journal 1988 February 25, pp 16–17
Professional indemnity insurance difficulties within the design-build contractors are assessed.

540
J. D. Allen
DESIGN & CONSTRUCT CAN OFFER CLIENTS A GUARANTEED PRICE
Construction News 1988 February 4, p20
An interview with the Chief Executive of the IDC Group which discussed how design & construct can offer a lump sum or GMP when only 15% of the design work has been completed.

1987

539
A. A. Montague
RESPONSIBILITIES OF A CONTRACTOR UNDER A DESIGN AND BUILD CONTRACT: THE DRAFTING OF THE CONTRACT FOR THE DOCKLANDS LIGHT RAILWAY
Proc. Liability of Contractors Conference 1984. Longman. 1987. pp 46–56

538
J. J. Goudsmit
LEGAL LIABILITY IN CONTRACT STRUCTURES
Proc. Liability of Contractors Conference 1984. Longman. 1987. pp 17-33
The implications are discussed of various contract structures for the liability of the contractor. Reference is made to contractors compliance with instructions, his duty to warn, failure of equipment, inviting alternative tenders, limitations on liability, delay, turnkey contracts, design, variations, nominated sub-contractors and choice of materials.

537
M. Furmston
LIABILITY OF CONTRACTORS: PRINCIPLES AND LIABILITY IN CONTRACT AND TORT
Proc. Liability of Contractors Conference 1984. Longman. 1987. pp 10-16

536
Royal Institution of Chartered Surveyors
PROJECT MANAGEMENT IN PROPERTY DEVELOPMENT
1987. pp 19
A promotional booklet extolling the virtues of quantity surveyors as project managers.

535
S. Rowlinson
DESIGN BUILD – ITS DEVELOPMENT AND PRESENT STATUS
CIOB Occasional Paper No 36. 1987. pp 16
The development is briefly examined of design build contracting, of the industry's perception of it and of its organisational forms and attributes. An assessment is made of the performance of design build projects based on over 40 detailed case studies.

534
C. J. Willis and A. Ashworth
PRACTICE AND PROCEDURE FOR THE QUANTITY SURVEYOR
1987. 9th edition. Collins. pp 249
The major revisions cover the changes affecting private practice and there is a new chapter on the QS's work in a construction firm. The growing importance of computers is acknowledged and there is a new chapter on project management.

533
L.C.N. Fan
EQUITY JOINT VENTURES IN THE CONSTRUCTION INDUSTRY IN CHINA
Occasional Paper No. 37. 1987. CIOB. pp 17
Following an outline of the construction industry in China attention is given to the formation and termination of equity joint ventures. This is followed by a case study illustrating the setting up of a services company. Appendices list the Chinese legislation relating to joint ventures.

532
S. Rowlinson
EXPERT SYSTEM DEVELOPMENT PROBLEMS IN PRACTICE
Proc. Application of Artificial Intelligence Techniques to Civil & Structural Engineering Conference. 1987. pp 7–13
The development is described for an expert system to advise on procurement strategy.

531
I. N. D. Wallace
TURNKEY CONTRACTS
Proc. Liability of Contractors Conference 1984.
Longman. 1987. pp 34–39

530
D. F. Turner
DESIGN & BUILD CONTRACT PRACTICE
1987. Longman. pp 264
The basis of design–build and the type of client and work
for which it is suited are discussed. Procedures to be followed are described and attention drawn to the requirements of each party and their consultants. In particular,
consideration is given to design responsibilities, possible
liabilities and financial arrangements. The text is linked to
the JCT contract with contractor's design, the BPF/ACA
system and obtaining design through nominated sub–contractors.

529
CIRIA
**PRACTICAL ADVICE FOR THE CLIENT INTENDING
TO BUILD**
Special Publication 48. 1987. pp 12

528
A. C. Sidwell and V. Ireland
**INTERNATIONAL COMPARISON OF CONSTRUC-
TION MANAGEMENT**
Australian Institute of Building Papers 1987 *2*, pp 3–11
The forms of construction management practised in Aus-
tralia, US and UK, including agency and direct con-
struction management, are defined and contrasted.

527
S. Rowlinson
**COMPARISON OF CONTRACTING SYSTEMS FOR
INDUSTRIAL BUILDINGS**
Managing Construction Worldwide. Volume 1. Systems
for managing construction. 1987. Spon/CIOB/ CIB. pp
55–65
A comparison is made of design-build and traditional
methods of procurement.

526
K. K. Bertli and Z. Herbsman
**CONSTRUCTION MANAGEMENT IS IT REALLY
THE WAY TO GO?**
Managing Construction Worldwide. Volume 1. Systems
for managing construction. 1987. Spon/CIOB/CIB.
pp 4–15
A comparative analysis is made of the Construction Man-
agement approach (US) to procurement to illustrate its
advantages and limitations.

525
S. G. Naoum and D. A Langford
MANAGEMENT CONTRACTING
Managing Construction Worldwide. Volume 1. Systems
for managing construction. 1987 Spon/CIOB/CIB. pp 42-
54
The relationship is evaluated between project success
and building procurement method in industrial and
commercial projects. A comparison is made between
management contracting and the traditional method of
procurement.

524
O. D. Wilson et al
**COMPETITIVE TENDERING: THE IDEAL NUMBER
OF TENDERS**
Managing Construction Worldwide. Volume 1. Systems
for managing construction. 1987. Spon/CIOB/CIB.
pp 175–186
The effect is examined of the number of bidders on the
outcome of the tendering process.

523
C. E Haltenhoff
**CONSTRUCTION MANAGEMENT PERFORMANCE
UNDER DUAL SERVICES AGREEMENTS**
ASCE Journal of Construction Engineeting & Manage-
ment 1987 *113* December, pp 640–647
The standard documents of the American Institute of
Architects and the Associated General Contractors of
America for construction management projects imply
processes and operational procedures that have become
customary if not standard since publication in 1975.
Adjustments must be made to accommodate the
particular form and variation of construction management specifically required by the contract. However,
construction management firms have a tendency to
customise processes and procedures for their own
convenience. This is especially true on projects where
a firm is contractually assigned other service responsibilities such as design, contracting, or construction. When a
CM process and its procedures exactly match the intent
of the project delivery system, owners are positioned
to gain from the use of the system. When convenience
intervenes, the system cannot function effectively, and
the owner may experience negative results. This paper
argues that convenient customizing of the CM process and
its procedures, especially customizing that mitigates the
checks and balances specifically built into the construction management system and implied by established CM
practice, represents a detrimental divergence from the
fundamental reasons CN is selected for use by owners on
their projects.

522
M. Branton & T. Butler
FIRM FOUNDATION FOR PROJECT MANAGEMENT
International Journal of Project Management 1987 *5*
November pp 221-229
The basic principles of project management are reviewed.

521
C. E. Haltenhoff
**CONSTRUCTION MANAGEMENT PERFORMANCE
UNDER DUAL SERVICES AGREEMENTS**
ASCE Journal of Construction Engineering & Man-
agement 1987 *113* December, pp 640–647
The standard documents of the American Institute of
Architects and the Associated General Contractors of
America for construction management projects imply
processes and operational procedures that have become
customary if not standard since publication in 1975.
Adjustments must be made to accommodate the particular form and variation of construction management
specifically required by the contract. However, construction management firms have a tendency to customise processes and procedures for their own convenience. This is especially true on projects where a
firm is contractually assigned other service responsibilities such as design, contracting, or construction. When

a CM process and its procedures exactly match the intent of the project delivery system, owners are positioned to gain from the use of the system. When convenience intervenes, the system cannot function effectively, and the owner may experience negative results. This paper argues that convenient customising of the CM process and its procedures, especially customising that mitigates the checks and balances specifically built into the construction management system and implied by established CM practice, represents a detrimental divergence from the fundamental reasons CM is selected for use by owners on their projects.

520
M. Branton & T. Butler
FIRM FOUNDATION FOR PROJECT MANAGEMENT
International Journal of Project Management 1987 5 November pp 221–229
The basic principles of project management are reviewed.

519
A. Catto
NEW CONTRACTS FOR OLD PROBLEMS
Building Today 1987 194 November 5, pp 22–24
A review of the current situation in management contracting and project management supplemented by personal observation. Reference is made to the imminent JCT form and the civil engineering form designed by Martin Barnes for the 'whole range of construction work'.

518
B. Meecham
FULL TIME SCORE FROM WATFORD
National Builder 1987 68 October, pp 330–331
The fast track construction by Dow–Mac design and build, of Watford's new football stand is outlined.

517
S. G. Naoum and D. Langford
MANAGEMENT CONTRACTING. THE CLIENT'S VIEW
ASCE Journal of Construction Engineering m Management 1987 113 (3) September, pp 369–385
The development of and the market for management contracting in the UK is summarised. The results are reported of interviews with construction clients who are asked to compare management contracting with the traditional method of project procurement.

516
MANAGEMENT CONTRACTING ON THE BRITISH TELECOM BUILDING
Construction 1987 (61) September, pp 52–55
Aspects discussed include design brief, contract selection, organisation and responsibilities, and costs and control procedures.

515
A. Westbrook
MANAGEMENT CONTRACTING THE CLIENT'S EVALUATION
Building Technology & Management 1987 25 August/September. p 17

514
P Gregory
MANAGEMENT CONTRACTING – THE RECKONING
Building Techology & Management 1987 25 August/September, pp 18–22
Consideration is given to the way the cost of a management contract is constituted and the comparison of that figure with perceived cost of the project at inception.

513
J. McKenna
MANAGEMENT CONTRACTING DEFINING THE SYSTEM
Building Techology & Management 1987 25 August/September, pp 23-25

512
R. Knowles
MANAGEMENT CONTRACTING / LAW AND CONTRACT
Building Techology & Management 1987 25 August/September, pp 26–27, 30

511
T. Scott
ARE CONTRACTORS MORE EFFICIENT AT BILL PRODUCTION?
Chartered Quantity Surveyor 1987 9 August, p15
Experience within a design and build organisation is reported.

510
CLIENT PARTICIPATION. MANAGEMENT BY DESIGN
Architects Journal 1987 186 August 19 & 26, pp 68–71
IBM's project management approach to its procurement of buildings is outlined.

509
R. Swan
DESIGN & BUILD
Contract Journal 1987 July 30, pp 12-13
A review of the place and importance of design and build.

508
M. Kemp
APPLICATION OF QUALITY ASSURANCE IN A PROJECT MANAGEMENT PRACTICE
Chartered Quantity Surveyor 1987 9 June, pp 25–26

507
WHAT PRICE PROJECT MANAGEMENT?
Chartered Quantity Surveyor 1987 9 June, p28
The problems are discussed of professional indemnity insurances for project management companies.

506
C. Sayer and J. Sutton
BPF SYSTEM
Chartered Quantity Surveyor 1987 9 June, pp 30–31
Experience is reported which was gained on a refurbishment project

505
B. Martin
ALLOCATING THE RISK
Building 1987 *252* June 12, p25
The risks likely to be assumed by a management contractor are discussed. It is suggested that future construction management arrangements should focus more on opportunities for improving management and less on assigning risks.

504
P. Reina
CHANGING THE RULES
Contract Journal 1987 May 21, pp 14–15
Some personal views are expressed on the relative merits of management contracting and construction management.

503
S. MacVicar
SMALL BEGINNINGS
Contract Journal 1987 May 7, p16
Portrait of Genesis Design & Construct, a subsidiary of Sir Robert McAlpine & Sons.

502
CASE STUDY. MAKING THE GRADE AT BEVIS MARKS HOUSE
Building Technology & Management 1987 *25* April/May, pp 14–19
Fast track construction of the seven storey building let under a management contract is described, particular attention being given to project organisation, production and quality control, and financial control.

501
T. Ostler
BUILDING A REPUTATION
Building Design 1987 April 17, pp 14–16
A profile of J. T. Design Build based in Bristol.

500
A. S. White and M. Barnes
ROLES AND RESPONSIBILITIES UNDER THE BPF SYSTEM
Structural Engineer 1987 *65A* March, pp 90–94

499
QUALIFICATION AND SELECTION OF CONSTRUCTION MANAGERS WITH SUGGESTED GUIDELINES FOR SELECTION PROCESS
ASCE Journal of Construction Engineering & Management 1987 *113* (1) March, pp 51–89
CM is a unique alternative system of contracting that competes with the general contracting and design–build contracting systems as a means of delivering projects. The CM system breaks down into several forms that have separate variations. CM services are provided by construction managers using different practitioner formats. In essence, CM services comprise a menu from which a form and its variation are selected. For these reasons, clients often have difficulty understanding the service available and determining the combination of services that best suits their requirements when engaging a construction manager. The guidelines presented are in fundamental form in order to accommodate both first–time users of CM services and repeat users seeking additional CM information.

498
C. S. Tyler
CONSTRUCTION MANAGEMENT CONTRACT AND THE ROLE OF THE ENGINEER
Structural Engineer 1987 *65A* March, pp 96–98

497
J. Robinson
COMPARISON OF TENDERING PROCEDURES AND CONTRACTUAL ARRANGEMENTS
Project Management 1987 *5* February, pp 19–24
The results are compared of the traditional procurement stages of a multistage industrial development and a package deal. Time over–runs and cost increases were much greater with the former.

496
R. Slavid
RESERVATIONS, BUT HEALTHY GROWTH IN DESIGN AND BUILDING
Construction News 1987 February 19, pp 13–14
An analysis is made of the market, advantages and limitations of design build based on a survey of contractors, designers, QSs and clients.

494
J. Bennett
CONSTRUCTION MANAGEMENT AND THE CHARTERED QUANTITY SURVEYOR
1986. Surveyors Press. pp 48
Following a review of the state of construction management practice, attention is given to the advice which quantity surveyors might give to clients wishing to adopt the approach to procurement. Finally, practical steps to be taken by the PQS wishing to offer a construction management service are indicated.

493
P. W. G. Morris
PROJECT MANAGEMENT: A VIEW FROM OXFORD
International Journal of Construction Management & Technology 1986 *1* (1), pp 36–52
Work on project success and failure is reviewed and factors associated with success are identified.

492
I. N. D. Wallace
CONSTRUCTION AND CONTRACTS: PRINCIPLES AND POLICIES IN TORT AND CONTRACT
1986. Sweet & Maxwell. pp 696
An extensive coverage of contractual issues under the main headings of new developments in the law; contractors claims and owners damages; certificates and their effect; guarantees and bonds; nominated sub-contractors; choice of contracting arrangements; comparative law; JCT standard forms; and Singapore SIA contract.

1986

491
J. W. Birnie
ECONOMIC EFFICIENCY OF CONSTRUCTION
Building Technology & Management 1986 *24* December, pp12–13
It is shown how traditional procurement kept unit costs of construction low.

490
A. Morris
INSPIRATION FOR QS DIVERSIFICATION
Chartered Quantity Surveyor 1986 *9* November, pp 23–25
The construction management (CM) approach to procurement in the US is described

489
PROJECT MANAGEMENT
Chartered Surveyor Weekly 1986 *17* November 27, pp 893–894, 897, 900, 903, 908, 911
A series of articles is presented including
  The men on the spot explain by G. Parker
  Who makes a building happen? by J. Thornton
  The building surveyor as project manager by M. Ridley
  Picking the man for the job by H. Evans
  American way is best by R. Catt
  The multi-disciplinary man by J. Fitton
  Tenant benefits from early involvement in a project by G. Parker

488
L. D. Phillips
CM CERTIFICATION AND REGISTRATION
Proceedings ASCE Convention on Construction Management, Boston, Mass. October, 27, 1986, pp 89–101
The present legal status of the CM system is reviewed from the perspective of a survey of 50 US states. A look is taken at the efforts to professionalise the construction manager's role in the industry.

487
L. S. Rigg
EDUCATIONAL PROGRAMMES SUPPORTING THE CM SYSTEM
Proceedings ASCE Convention on Construction Management, Boston, Mass. October 27, 1986, pp 62–73
The differences are established between the educational requirements of a contracting oriented programme and a CM oriented programme with respect to the management tools and the philosophy of using those tools.

486
W. C. Kwasny
QUALITY IN THE CM CONSTRUCTED PROJECT
Proceedings ASCE Convention on Construction Management, Boston, Mass. October 27, 1986, pp 74–80
It is shown that the services of a testing laboratory are an essential requirement of the CM quality management system.

485
F. Muller
CM's EXPOSURE TO LIABILITY
Proceedings ASCE Convention on Construction Management, Boston, Mass. October 27, 1986, pp 117–133
Attention is given to contractual relationships, standard of care.

484
C. E. Haltenhoff
FORMS AND VARIATIONS OF THE CM SYSTEM
Proceedings ASCE Convention on Construction Management, Boston, Mass. October 27, 1986, pp 1–15
In the CM system, the independent contractor relationship inherent in general contracting and in design build, is altered by substituting a fiduciary/agent construction manager. The construction manager is responsible for all aspects of project delivery, the owner becoming, in effect, his own contractor, retaining or assigning the various risks. The various forms of CM are described from a contract perspective.

483
C. Kluenker
BROAD SPECTRUM OF CM SERVICES
Proceedings ASCE Convention on Construction Management, Boston, Mass. October 27, 1986, pp 16–50
Basic CM tools viz computer systems; documents and techniques; people and the organisation; and CM industry associations, are discussed. Reference is made to contract risks, budgets, programmes, payments, meetings and bidding documents. Job descriptions are given for project manager and CM co–ordinator.

482
P. S. Scott and W. E. Showalter
HISTORY OF CONSTRUCTION MANAGEMENT
Proceedings ASCE Convention on Construction Management, Boston, Mass. October 27, 1986, pp 51–61
The highlights are traced of the development of CM.

481
C. E. Haltenhoff
CM MULTIPLE CONTRACTING COST MODEL
Proceedings ASCE Convention on Construction Management, Boston, Mass. October 27, 1986, pp 81–88
The economic advantages are demonstrated of CM when a multiple contracting format is utilised, which are based on actual data collected during the bidding of such contracts.

480
F. Roberts
MORE POWER TO THE ESTIMATOR'S ELBOW
Construction Computing 1986 (15) October, pp 14–15
Lesser Design & Build's experience with Techsonix computer systems for taking off, bill generation, estimates and schedules to final accounts is summarised.

479
BPF CONTRACT: THE PROFESSIONALS VERDICT
Construction News 1986 October 23, pp 28–29
A round table discussion is reported on the BPF system.

478
C. Wist
DESIGN/BUILD METHODS MATURE
Architecture 1986 October, pp 107–109

477
L. Parnell
PROJECT MANAGEMENT: WHO IS RESPONSIBLE?
Chartered Surveyor Weekly 1986 *16* September 25, p900f
Liability in project management is discussed.

476
S. M. Rowlinson & R. Newcombe
INFLUENCE OF PROCUREMENT FORM ON PROJECT PERFORMANCE
Proc CIB 10th Triennal Congress. Washington. September 1986 Volume 8. pp 3592–3599
A comparison is made primarily between design–build and traditional.

475
D. W. Birchall and M. C. Bottjer
MANAGEMENT CONTRACTING. THE VIEWS OF GENERAL CONTRACTORS
Building Technology & Management 1986 *24* August/September, pp 40–43,49
The results are reported of a survey of medium sized contractors to establish their intentions regarding management contracting, how they were organised to cope and how they viewed its future.

474
J. G. Perry and R. W. Hayes
RISK MANAGEMENT FOR PROJECT MANAGERS
Building Technology & Management 1986 *24* August/September, pp 8–11
The various stages of risk management are considered, prior to an analysis of the ways it can be used throughout a project.

473
F. Mastrandrea
LIABILITY OF THE CONSTRUCTION PROJECT MANAGER
Construction Management & Economics 1986 *4* Autumn, pp 105–134
A framework is developed of areas of potential civil liability of the consultant project manager. The basic principles of contract, agency and torts of negligence are explored and analogies for project management drawn. The developed principles are tested against several decisions in the USA.

472
R. Knowles
PROJECT MANAGER: LEGAL POSITION
Chartered Quantity Surveyor 1986 *8* August, p6
The relevant areas of the law are considered which are relevant to the project manager's responsibilities.

471
J. Franks
CONTRACT WITHOUT COMBAT
Building 1986 *261* August 15, pp 37–40
The application is described of the BPF system to an office refurbishment.

470
R. Ormerod et al
PROJECT MANAGEMENT REVIEW PART 2
Construction Computing 1986 (14) July, pp 25–37

469
R. Knowles
PROJECT MANAGER: THE LEGAL POSITION, PART 1
Chartered Quantity Surveyor 1986 *8* July, p11
The legal responsibilities are considered with reference to relevant case law.

468
M. E. Schneider
TURNKEY CONTRACTS. CONCEPT, LIABILITIES, CLAIMS
International Construction Law Review 1986 *3* July, pp 338–359

467
E. A. Schwartz
DISPUTES BETWEEN JOINT VENTURERS: A CASE STUDY
International Construction Law Review 1986 *3* July, pp 360–374
Following a discussion of the background to the dispute, certain aspects of the arbitration procedure are reviewed. In conclusion the most interesting aspects of the award are examined.

466
R. Hayes
WHO CARRIES THE RISK?
Building Technology & Management 1986 *24* June, pp 42–45
The risk elements of management contracting are considered.

465
G. Vickers
PRACTICE EDUCATION. PROJECT MANAGEMENT
Architects Journal 1986 *183* June 25, pp 75–76

464
A. Hunter
PROJECT MANAGEMENT: DEFINING THE TERMS
Chartered Quantity Surveyor 1986 *8* June, pp 20–21
Some misconceptions in relation to project management, construction management and management contracting are dispelled.

463
J. D. Allen
CONSTRUCTION MANAGEMENT KEEPS BROADGATE ON FAST TRACK
Construction News 1986 April 3, pp 22–25
The management contracting approach is providing a fast track operation. Some of the management issues are discussed.

462
J. G. Perry
DEALING WITH RISK IN CONTRACTS
Building Technology & Management 1986 *24* April, pp23–26
The relationship between type of contract viz lump sum, and measurement, target cost, and cost reimbursable and risk is discussed.

461
M. Taylor
PRACTICE CONTRACTS. TENDERING
Architects Journal 1986 *183* April 23, pp 61–62
The code for design and build and advice on joint venture tendering issued by the NJCC are reviewed.

460
M. R. Morris
CONSTRUCTION MANAGEMENT. US INSPIRATION FOR QS DIVERSIFICATION
Paper to RICS Annual Conference, March 1986. pp 14
Construction management services in the USA provide management of cost, time and quality, with direct responsibility to the client. Its advantages are discussed.

459
D. Brooks
DOES PUBLIC ACCOUNTABILITY ACHIEVE VALUE FOR MONEY
Building Technology & Management 1986 *24* March, pp 11–14
The relative merits are compared of the various means of procurement.

458
N. Morrison
CONTRACT NEWS
Chartered Quantity Surveyor 1986 *8* January, pp 14–15
The results are presented of a survey as to the use of various forms of contract in 1984. Some data are presented on the forms of procurement employed related to size of project.

457
POLITICAL OBSTACLE COURSE TESTS PROJECT MANAGEMENT AND TURNKEY
Contract Journal 1986 *329* January 16, pp 14–16
The success of the Docklands Light Railway project is claimed to result from the appointment of a project management team to handle the contract and the letting of the contract on a turnkey basis. Main points of the contract provisions are summarised.

1985

456
D. Hobson
MANAGEMENT CONTRACTING. A STEP IN THE RIGHT DIRECTION
1985. Surveyors Publications. pp 30
Consideration is given to the benefits of management contracting and to the role of the QS.

455
G. D. G. Cottam
MANAGEMENT CONTRACTING AND PACKAGE DEALS
Proc. Supervision of Construction Symposium. ICE. London. 7–8 June 1984.
1985. Telford. pp 51–58; Discussion pp 79–88

454
National Joint Consultative Committee
CODE OF PROCEDURE FOR SELECTIVE TENDERING FOR DESIGN AND BUILD
1985. RIBA Publications. pp 11

453
National Joint Consultative Committee
JOINT VENTURE TENDERING FOR CONTRACTS IN THE UK
1985. RIBA Publications. pp 4

452
Construction Industry Research and Information Association
CLIENTS GUIDE TO COST REIMBURSABLE CONTRACTS IN BUILDING
1985. pp 12

451
I. Pennington
GUIDE TO THE BPF SYSTEM AND CONTRACT
1985. CIOB. pp 36
A commentary on the BPF manual is followed by details of the BPF/ACA form of building agreement.

450
P. A. Thompson
CONTRACTUAL ASPECTS OF INFRASTRUCTURE RENOVATION
Conference paper. 1985. pp 8
The major forms of procurement are outlined.

449
G. Gosney
MANAGEMENT PROJECTIONS
Building 1985 *269* December 6. pp 38–39
A profile of Project Management International

448
P. Bil
CHEOPS MANAGEMENT PROJECTIONS
Building 1985 *269* December 13. pp 36–37
A profile of Cheops project management services offered by a quantity surveying practice.

447
R. Hayes
RISKS OF MANAGEMENT CONTRACTING
Chartered Quantity Surveyor 1985 *8* December. pp 197–198

446
B. Waters
SCHAL INTERNATIONAL MANAGEMENT PROJECTIONS
Building 1985 *269* December 20 27 pp 18–19
A profile of the project management consultancy.

445
H. Nahapiet and J. Nahapiet
COMPARISON OF CONTRACTUAL ARRANGEMENTS FOR BUILDING PROJECTS
Construction Management and Economics 1985 *3* (3) Winter, pp 217–231
Contracts are considered from an organisational perspective, comparing the major forms of contracts available for building projects and examining the factors influencing their selection. The analysis is based on the findings of a study of ten building projects, six in the USA and four in the UK, together with the results of a survey of those prominent in the industry. A comparison of five different contractual arrangements indicates that they establish different patterns of responsibilites and relationships between clients and the various parties involved in building projects. In so doing, they are regarded as offering clients differing combinations of expertise, risk, flexibility and costs. For the projects studied, three factors were found to be related to contract selection: the characteristics of clients, particularly their experience and expertise in construction, the level of performance required by clients and the construction complexity of projects. These findings, together with previous research, suggest that it is unlikely that there is one 'best' form of contract of building projects. Rather, which is the appropriate contractual arrangement varies

according to the particular set of project circumstances, especially the type of client, his time and cost requirements and the characteristics of the project.

444
J. S McArthur
SHARPENING THE CLAUSES
Chartered Quantity Surveyor 1985 *8* November pp 146–148
The reasons are considered why the Scottish scparatc trades contracting system is now in disuse, being replaced by the all trade contract.

443
MANAGEMENT CONTRACTING CREATES NEW VICTIMS OF UNFAIR TERMS
Contract Journal 1985 *327* October 17, p 13
The growth of onerous contract conditions, particularly in regard to management contracting, is discussed.

442
G. Bushell
ALTERNATIVE MANAGEMENT IN NORTHAMPTON
Chartered Quantity Surveyor 1985 *8* September. pp 50–51
A separate trades approach to the construction of a factory extension is described.

441
N. Fisher
PROJECT MANAGEMENT EDUCATION IN THE 1990s
Building Techology & Management 1985 *23* September. pp 10–12
The Project Management Master's course at Reading University is described.

440
J. Ratcliffe
PROJECT MANAGEMENT
Estates Gazette 1985 *275* August 17, pp 620–622: August 24, pp 707–709; August 31, pp 791–793; September 7, pp 862, 864–865; September 14, pp 1000–1001
The role of the project manager is established under the headings of total project management; funding; procurement; marketing; and the future.

439
R. Judson
DUCTWORKERS SHOULD LOVE MANAGEMENT CONTRACTS
Building Services 1985 *7* July, p 55
The advantages of management contracting to ductwork contractors are identified.

438
D. Birchall and R. Newcombe
DEVELOPING THE SKILLS
Chartered Quantity Surveyor 1985 *7* July, pp 472–473
The qualities required of the project manager are discussed.

437
D. Dibb-Fuller
DESIGN AND BUILD USING COMPUTERS
Construction Computing 1985 July (10), pp 37–39
Experience of Conder in using the CADAM system is reported.

436
D. H. T. Walker
PROJECT MANAGEMENT IN PERSPECTIVE
Construction Computing 1985 (11) Autumn. pp 14–16
Information systems are identified for project management at the feasibility, design and construction stages.

435
C. Kluenker
CONSTRUCTION MANAGEMENT EXPLODING SOME MYTHS
American Professional Constructor 1985 *9* June. pp 2–4
Construction management is defined on the bringing of construction expertise to the project team during all phases of project delivery, beginning with conceptual design.

434
B. Owens
CONSTRUCTION A CLIENT'S VIEWPOINT
Building Economist 1985 *24* June. pp 17–20
The role and responsibility of the project manager are discussed, particular reference being made to value management and life cycle costing.

433
D. Summers
BPF SYSTEM
Building Economist 1985 *24* June. pp 2–9
The salient points of the system are examined, its implications for quantity surveyors being summarised.

432
D. Birchall and R. Newcombe
LEARNING FROM EXPERIENCE
Chartered Quantity Surveyor 1985 *7* June, pp 436–437
Results are presented of a survey of the problem areas facing project managers.

430
J. D. Allen
BROADGATE MOVING ON FAST TRACK
Construction News 1985 June 27, p14
The client's reasons for appointing a construction manager for a property development project are outlined. Disenchantment with the JCT forms and bills of quantity appear to be two.

429
J. Bale
TRAINING FOR A NEW AGE
Building 1985 *268* May 24, pp 38–39
The demands that management contracting places on training both in higher education and on-the-job are discussed.

428
J. Osborne
CITY IN THE MAKING
Building 1985 *268* May 3, pp 36–41
Brief details are given of a fast track office development – London Bridge City – let on a construction management (management contracting) contract.

427
M. Bar-Hillel
MASTER OF ALL TRADES?
Chartered Surveyor Weekly 1985 *11* April 11, pp 115–116
The case is made for the QS as project manager.

426
G. Hardwick
CONTROL AND IN-HOUSE EXPERTISE SELL: IDC DESIGN AND CONSTRUCT
Contract Journal 1985 *324* april 11, pp 20–21
A portrait of IDC and the success of its Guaranteed Maximum Price Contract

425
MANAGEMENT MEASURES UP
Building 1985 *268* March 1, pp 30–31
The salient points are presented of a survey into the use of management contracting and the response by architects, clients and QSs. The top 16 management contractors are listed.

424
CASE STUDY – NO NEED FOR SUPER MANAGERS
Construction Computing 1985 (8) January, pp 22–24
Computer use is outlined for a design and manage project by Kyle Stewart involving a site work force of 200 from a complete range of sub–contractors.

1984

423
J. A. Armitt
JOINT VENTURES FORMATION AND OPERATION
Proceedings ICE Conference 'Management of Construction Projects' London. November 1984. Thomas Telford. pp 61–71; Discussion pp 95–102

422
F. R. Donovan
TURNKEY PROJECTS
Proceedings ICE Conference 'Management of Construction Projects' London. November 1984. Thomas Telford. pp 45–59; Discussion. pp 95–102
The essential elements of a turnkey project are outlined.

421
J. R. Elton
MANAGEMENT CONTRACTING
Proceedings ICE Conference 'Management of Construction Projects' London. November 1084. Thomas Telford. pp 73–83; Discussion pp 95–102
The essential elements of management contracting are described.

420
B. Waters
CENTRE OF DEBATE
Building 1984 *267* November 16, pp 37–46
The operational performance of the PSA management contract for the construction of the International Conference Centre is one aspect discussed. Another is the Artemis computer based programming and progressing system.

419
E. Haltenhoff
INNOVATIVE CONTRACTING A TREND
American Professional Constructor 1984 *8* Winter, pp 6–10
The four variant forms of construction management as practiced in the US are described.

418
R.Knowles
MORE ON THE BPF AGREEMENT
Chartered Quantity Surveyor 1984 *7* September, p51
Attention is given to additional drawings; named sub-contractors and supp liers; commencement and delay; final certificate and release of retention; termination; fluctuations; and arbitration.

417
J. Rawlinson
PROJECT MANAGEMENT A QUANTITY SURVEYING VIEWPOINT
Building Economist 1984 *24* September, pp 17–21

416
A. Walker and W. P Hughes
PRIVATE INDUSTRIAL PROJECT MANAGEMENT: A SYSTEMS-BASED CASE STUDY
Construction Management and Economics 1984 *2* Autumn, pp 93–109
The technique of linear responsibility analysis is used for a retrospective case study of a private industrial development consisting of an extension to existing buildings to provide a warehouse, services block and packing line. The organisational structure adopted on the project is analyses using concepts from systems theory which are included in Walker's theoretical model of the structure of building project organisations (Walker, 1981). This model proposes that the process of building provision can be viewed as systems and subsystems which are differentiated from each other at decision points. Further to this, the subsystems can be viewed as the interaction of managing system and operating system. Using Walker's model, a systematic analysis of the relationships between the contributors gives a quantitative assessment of the efficacy of the organisational structure used. The causes of the client's dissatisfaction with the outcome of the project were lack of integration and complexity of the managing system. However, there was a high level of satisfaction with the completed project and this is reflected by the way in which the organisation structure corresponded to the model's propositions.

415
R. Owens
CAMBRIDGE COST CUTTER
Architects Journal 1984 *180* August 15, p18
A local authority has let a concrete framed office block

to a develop and construct builder. It has produced significant savings by introducing a competitive element into the structural design.

414

V. Ireland

VIRTUALLY MEANINGLESS DISTINCTIONS BETWEEN NOMINALLY DIFFERENT PROCUREMENT METHODS

Proc 4th Int. Symposium on Organisation and Management of Construction. Waterloo. Canada. July 1984. pp 203–211

The procurement methods of lump sum, provisional quantities and reimbursement, package deal, construction management and project management are considered in terms of cost determining contractor selection; specialists roles; process structure and contract conditions.

413

S. M. Rowlinson and R. Newcombe

COMPARISON OF PROCUREMENT FORMS FOR INDUSTRIAL BUILDINGS IN THE UK

Proc, 4th Int Symposium on Organisation and Management and Construction. Waterloo. Canada. July 1984. pp 247–256

A framework is set out within which the client and contractor conceptions of project performance can be assessed. The assessment takes place within the context of the forms of procurement currently available.

412

A. C Sidwell

MEASUREMENT OF SUCCESS OF VARIOUS ORGANISATIONAL FORMS FOR CONSTRUCTION PROJECTS

Proc 4th Int Symposium on Organisation and Management of Construction. Waterloo. Canada July 1984. pp 283–289

The problems are discussed of evaluating project success and the performance of various organisational forms is examine in terms of cost time and quality.

411

T. N. D. Wallace

CONTRACTS FOR INDUSTRIAL PLANT PROJECTS

International Construction Law Review 1984 *1* July pp 322–355

Attention is given to methods of procurement including turnkey, separate contracts, joint ventures and project management and methods of payment.

410

M. W. Chin

ASSESSMENT OF ALTERNATIVE MANAGEMENT APPROACHES TO CONSTRUCTION PROJECTS IN THE WEST INDIES

Paper to CIB W–65 4th International Symposium on Organisation and Management of Construction. Waterloo, Canada. July 1984. Vol 4. pp 1343–1350

The paper reviews the current alternative management approaches to construction projects in the West Indies and discusses the problems and prospects of the various delivery systems in relation to a number of projects in the West Indies. Particular attention is given to the professional construction management (PCM) approach which has been emerging in the West Indies in recent years as a viable alternative to the traditional approach for the successful completion of construction projects. Some of the potential legal problems of using such an approach are highlighted. The paper concludes with an assessment of the advantages and disadvantages of the various delivery systems in the light of the results of ten case studies undertaken in Trinidad and Tobago.

409

S. G. Naoum and D. A. Langford

MANAGEMENT CONTRACTING A REVIEW OF THE SYSTEM

Proc. 4th Int. Symposium on Organisation and Management of Construction, Waterloo, Canada, July 1984, Volume 3, pp 1001–1013

408

J. Andrews

CONSTRUCTION PROJECT MANAGEMENT IN JOINT VENTURE IN DEVELOPING COUNTRIES

Proc. 4th Int. Shymposium on Organisation and Management of Construction. Waterloo, Canada, July 1984. Volume 3, pp 687–696

Following a restatement of reservations concerning joint ventures, attention is drawn to the growing and ill advised use of joint ventures in developing countries. Finally, some key aspects of management and organisation are outlined.

407

M. R. Baker and R. W Cockfield

INTERNATIONAL TURNKEY PROJECTS THE RISKS AND METHODS OF IMPACT REDUCTION

Proc. 4th Int. Symposium on Organisation and Management of Construction, Waterloo, Canada, July 1984, pp 17–29

406

C. E. E. Haltenhoff

CM (CONSTRUCTION MANAGEMENT): THE STATE OF THE ART

Proc. 4th Int. Symposium on Organisation and Management of Construction, Waterloo, Canada, July 1984. pp 179–191

405

E. O. O. Sawacha and D. A. Langford

PROJECT MANAGEMENT AND THE PUBLIC SECTOR CLIENT FOUR CASE STUDIES

Proc. 4th Int. Symposium on Organisation and Management of Construction. Waterloo, Canada, July 1984, pp 273–282

The use is investigated of project management for four public sector clients.

404

K. D. Waagenaar

TOTAL MANAGEMENT AN ADVANCED APPROACH TO PROJECT MANAGEMENT

Proc. 4th Int. Symposium on Organisation and Management of Construction, Waterloo, Canada, July 1984, pp 310–319

403
O. Oberti
PROJECT MANAGEMENT BY PROFESSIONALS: CORRECT PROCEDURES AND PITFALLS
Proc. 4th Int. Symposium on Organisation and Management of Construction, Waterloo, Canada, July 1984, pp 235–245
The value of the professional as a project manager is discussed. An outline of the fundamentals of the approach and procedures required for successful project management is combined with an insight into the key ingredients of the contractual arrangements.

402
H. R. Thomas et al
GUIDELINES FOR THE DEVELOPMENT OF AUTHORITY STRUCTURES FOR HEAVY INDUSTRIAL CONSTRUCTION PROJECTS
Proc. 4th Int. Symposium on Organisation and Management of Construction, Waterloo, Canada, July 1984, pp 87–98
The organisational forms of project management are described and principles presented that related project characteristics to the best ???? of a project management structure. Guiding principles in the establishment and responsibilty and the location of the project manager within the hierarchy of the organisation are also outlined.

401
R. K. Stocks and S. P Male
INVESTIGATION INTO THE CLIENT'S PERCEPTIONS OF CONTRACTUAL FORMS AND PROCEDURES: THE INSTIGATION OF GOOD PRACTICE
Proc. 4th Int. Symposium on Organisation and Management of Construction, Waterloo, Canada, July 1984, pp 291–298
Contractual arrangements are considered in terms of the value of the client, it being concluded that they are over emphasised. More attention should be given to organisational procedures, including communication, co-ordination, reporting procedures and impersonal relationships.

400
S. Goth
CONSTRUCTION MANAGEMENT AND CONTROL OVER THE CONSTRUCTION LABOUR PROCESS
Proceedings 1983 Bartlett International Summer School. Geneva. 1984. pp 4–3—4–7
The ramifications of management contracting for industrial relations and safety are considered.

399
G. E Ninos and S. H. Wearne
RESPONSIBILITIES FOR PROJECT CONTROL DURING CONSTRUCTION. A GUIDE TO THE PROMOTERS AND CUSTOMERS OF BUILDING AND CIVIL ENGINEERING PROJECTS ON ORGANISATING THE CONTROL OF COST, QUALITY AND THE SPEED OF CONSTRUCTION
1984. School of Technological Management, University of Bradford. pp 74
Limitations on conventional means for controlling a construction project are considered to be capable of resolution by the use of a project manager (director). The project director has the responsibility and authority to make or delegate all decisions needed to achieve the project objectives within the target costs and completion time authorised.

398
A. Walker
PROJECT MANAGEMENT IN CONSTRUCTION
1984. Granada. pp 206
Designed to provoke a re-evaluation of the effectiveness of the organisation structures used in the management of construction projects. The client's role is distinguished and examined and a model of the construction process is developed, as is a method of analysing and designing project organisation structures. Against this backcloth a variety of organisational forms available for the implementation and management of construction projects are considered in terms of their contribution to the fulfilment of the client's objectives.

397
J. Franks
BUILDING PROCUREMENT SYSTEMS A GUIDE TO BUILDING PROJECT MANAGEMENT
1984. CIOB. pp 71
The various non-traditional forms (including BPF) of contracting are considered in turn, the advantages and limitations of each being identified. This is then followed by a comparative assessment. Finally there is a section of literature covering all systems.

396
R. F. Moore
RESPONSE TO CHANGE THE DEVELOPMENT OF NON-TRADITIONAL FORMS OF CONTRACTING
CIOB Occasional Paper No 31. 1984. pp 26
A resume is given of the reasons underlying the change from traditional to non-traditional forms of contracting having greater contractor involvement. Particular attention is paid to design build, turnkey and management contracting. The response of firms to these new techniques is evaluated by means of a survey which provides some hard data on the uptake.

395
Construction Industry Research and Information Association
A CLIENT'S GUIDE TO MANAGEMENT CONTRACTS IN BUILDING
1984. pp 12

394
BPF SYSTEM
Building 1984 *266* June 15. pp 28–33
Contributions on the new system of building management cover the advantages/limitations, the philosophy of the adapted ACA form for use with BPF systems and application of the system to two real projects.

393
B. D. Phillis
QUANTITY SURVEYOR AS PROJECT MANAGER
Building Economist 1984 *23* June, pp 7–9
The skill requirements of a project manager are compared to those of a quantity surveyor.

392
R. A. Hartland
PROJECT MANAGEMENT TODAY
Consulting Engineer 1984 June, pp 18–19
The changing role is examined of the project manager and
how he copes with the conflicting interests of the design
team and client.

391
M. R. K. Garnett
JOINT VENTURES Arbitration 1984 *49* May.
pp 326–331
The basic principles of joint ventures are outlined.

390
T. A. N. Precott et al
**FOYLE BRIDGE: ITS HISTORY, AND THE STRAT-
EGY OF THE DESIGN AND BUILD CONCEPT**
Proc. ICE 1984 *76* (1) May, pp 351–361
The history of the River Foyle crossings and the events
leading up to the decision to go to a design and build
contract are outlined. How the contract was drawn up,
the bids received and the assessment of the tenders and
the award of the contract are described.

389
T. A. N. Prescott et al
**FOYLE BRIDGE: ITS HISTORY, AND THE
STRATEGY OF THE DESIGN AND BUILD CON-
CEPT**
Proc. ICE 1984 *76* (1) May. pp 351–361
The history of the River Foyle crossings and the events
leading up to the decision to go to a design and build
contract are outlined. How the contract was drawn up,
the bids received and the assessment of the tenders and
the award of the contract are described.

388
B. P. Wex et al
**FOYLE BRIDGE: DESIGN AND TENDER IN A
DESIGN AND BUILD COMPETITION**
ICE Proc. 1984 *76* (1) May. pp 363–386
The positions are described of the contractor and designer
in design and build tender procedures and compares them
with their respective roles under normal UK tendering
practice. The setting up of the R.D.L. Graham Joint
Venture for the construction of the bridge is also covered.

387
L. Stace
BPF SYSTEM A PERSONAL VIEW
Chartered Surveyor Weekly 1984 7 April 5, p29
It is argued that the BPF approach is wrong in trying to
eliminate BOQ since it is the contract which is at fault.

386
J. Pain
CONCENTRATING THE CONTRACTOR'S MIND
Building 1984 *226* April 27, pp 32–33
Arguments are made to demonstrate the inadequacies of
traditional forms of contracting. Greater responsibility
for the contractor would encourage finishing the job on
time.

385
W. H. Alington
**COMMUNICATIONS FOR RUNNING MULTI-CON-
TRACT PROJECTS FROM A CONSULTANT'S
OFFICE**
Paper to AIB/NZIOB Conference 'Communication in
our industry', Christchurch, New Zealand, March 1984,
pp 75–84
The organisation of 'separate trades' contracts is
discussed with reference to the monitoring of the con-
tracts, the documentation and the supporting computer
systems.

384
H. Walton
PROJECT MANAGER A CAPITE AD CALCEM
Project Management 1984 *2* February, pp 31–35
The skills and qualities of a project manager are evaluated
in terms of the environments in which he may operate and
the tasks to be performed.

383
BPF SYSTEM
Building 1984 *266* June 15, pp 28–33
Contributions on the new system of building management
cover the advantages/limitations, the philosophy of
the adapted ACA form for use with the BPF system
and application of the system to two real projects.

382
B. P. Wex et al
**FOYLE BRIDGE: DESIGN AND TENDER IN A
DESIGN AND BUILD COMPETITION**
ICE Proc. 1984 *76* (1) May, pp 363–386
The positions are described of the contractor and designer
in design and build tender procedures and compares them
with their respective roles under normal UK Tendering
practice. The setting up of the R. D. L. Graham joint
venture for the construction of the bridge is also
covered.

381
A Sidwell
BUYING REFURBISHED BUILDINGS
Building Technology & Management 1984 *22* April,
pp 22–26
Means of procurement by traditional firm price contracts,
cost reimbursement contracts, management contracts,
single trades or AMM contracts, partnership agreements,
and serial contracts are discussed. A summary is provided
of the advantages and limitations of each

380
M. V. Manzoni
**PROJECT MANAGEMENT — NOW AND IN THE
FUTURE**
Paper to Chartered Quantity Surveyors 13th Triennial
Conference. London. April 1984. pp 17.
It is suggested that improvement of the industry will be
achieved only by means of an organisation structure
which ensures that each part of the industry provides
the development and training of its own discipline and
executes its own work without undue sub-letting. After
describing the principal contribution a contractor can
make a comparison is made of traditional contracting with
management contracting.

1983

379
C. Davies
EXHIBITION OF SPEED
Building 1984 *266* March 23, pp 30–32
Bovis's design-build approach to the construction of the Scottish Exhibition Centre is outlined.

378
B. Heaphy
BEHIND THE FEE SYSTEM
Building 1984 *266* March 16, pp 28–30
The advantages of the management fee contract are described.

377
L. Clements
KESSOCK BRIDGE DESIGN AND BUILD CON-TRACTS AND PROPOSALS FOR MANAGING SIMILAR CONTRACTS
ICE Proc. 1984 *76* (Part 1) February, pp 23–34
Events leading up to the planning and adoption of the design and build form of contract are reviewed. The aims, problems and achievements are described and proposals put forward for modified procedures which could be adopted for managing similar projects in the future.

376
H. Walton
PROJECT MANAGER A CAPITE AD CALCEM
Project Management 1984 *2* February, pp 31–35
The skills and qualities of a project manager are evaluated in terms of the environments in which he may operate and the tasks to be performed.

375
H. Try
AUNPALATABLE MEDICINE FOR THE BUILDING TEAM
Building Technology and Management 1984 *22* February, pp 3–4
A personal response to the British Property Federation's manual for building design and construction.

374
G. Testa
OLD ORDER CHANGETH. . . . ?
Chartered Quantity Surveyor 1984 *6* January, p 212
Two forms of non-traditional approach to contracting are outlined. One is a 'single source responsibility service' in which the clients spatial, functional, cost and time requirements are managed by the architect, with input from the contractor, until the main elements of the clients needs are established and the cost plan and programme frozen. Full responsibility then passes to the contractor with provision for input from the design team. The second approach involves a multi-disciplinary team with the general contractor as team leader in joint venture with a services contractor.

373
E. Haltenhoff
INNOVATIVE CONTRACTING A TREND
American Professional Constructor 1984 *8* Winter, pp 6–10
The four variant forms of construction management as practised in the US are described.

372
N. M. L. Barnes
BUILDING MORE FOR LESS – A COST AND PERFOR-MANCE STUDY
Proc. JLO Annual Conference 1983 'Building for recovery – new clients, new markets'. Birmingham, pp 3
Objectives of the study leading to the BPF manual are summarised.

371
R. W. Woodhead
METHODOLOGICAL APPROACH TO PROJECT MANAGEMENT
Proc. 9th CIB Congress. Stockholm 1983. Volume 1b. Renewal, rehabilitation and maintenance. pp 25–36
A methodological approach is presented to project management which focuses on the consideration of management functions, decision processes, and the role of managers. In this way basic project management concepts can be developed that have general validity.

370
W. J. Diepeveen
PROJECT MANAGEMENT AND ITS IMPACT ON THE MANAGEMENT OF PARTNER ORGANISA-TIONS
Proc. 9th CIB Congress. Stockholm 1983. Volume 1b. Renewal, rehabilitation and maintenance. pp 11–23
Project management wants to ensure efficient management of the construction process. It makes use of management techniques that guarantee the co-ordination of the activities of the different project partners such as the client, the architect, the consultants and the builder. The end result of a well organised construction process should be a building of optimum quality for the client. On the one hand the project partners should satisfy the needs of the client in a most effective way, but on the other hand they must keep an eye on the demands of continuity and rentability in their own organisations, be it an architects' partnership, a consultancy or engineering practice or a building firm. The best building may be harmful for the demands of their home organisation. Each partner has a divided responsibility, divided between his own interests and the interests of the client as seen through the eyes of a team of individual partners that may have never met before and who also may have conflicting interests. The two processes run simultaneously. Both the project and the partners organisations have their own demands for an effective management. The construction process asks for an optimum project management and the partners' own organisation at home must be guaranteed by an optimum business organisation. The two may come into conflict and we will see how the two may be developed in harmony and what measures will be needed to do it.

369
J. Bennett
PROJECT MANAGEMENT IN CONSTRUCTION
Construction Management and Economics 1983 *1* Winter, pp 183–197
A conceptual framework for project management in construction is proposed. It comprises two distinct phases. The first is strategic, being concerned with client objectives, project description and organisation. The second is

concerned with the execution of basic construction tasks. The essential nature of these concepts and of relationships between them is described. The need to regard projects as heirachies is discussed. The paper concludes that within construction projects, management, design and construction strategies must be matched and then given expression in clearly defined tasks. Creating and maintaining that consistent framework is project management.

368
R. Thomas et al
AUTHORITY STRUCTURES FOR CONSTRUCTION PROJECT MANAGEMENT
ASCE Journal of Construction Engineering and Management 1983 *109* (4) December, pp 406–422
A primer on authority structures is presented. The basic corporate organisational forms are described and construction examples are given. The basic authority structures for project management are also described. These forms are the functional, pure project, and matrix. For each form, the advantages and disadvantages as they relate to the project manager's ability to support the project are cited. Nine factors that influence the choice of authority structure are discussed. The role of the project manager is described. His effectiveness as a manager is related to the organisational form, hierarchy within the organisation, authority gap, management style, and the ability to resolve conflict. Six principles for developing a project organisation and selecting a project manager are given.

367
B. Waters
BPF SYSTEM
Building 1983 *265* December 16, pp 25–30
The main proposals of the British Property Federation in regard to procurement are described, the reasons underlying their introduction being outlined. A critique of the proposals is also included.

366
R. O. Powys
PROFESSIONAL CONSTRUCTION MANAGEMENT THE AUSTRALIAN PRIVATE SECTOR
Building Economist 1983 *22* December, pp 326–329
The concept is discussed of project management and management contracting reference being made to recruitment, fees and the position of the architect.

365
A. T. Brett-Jones
BARCHESTER LOW RISE: A CASE STUDY OF A MANAGEMENT CONTRACT FOR REMEDIAL WORK TO A LARGE HOUSING SCHEME
Construction Management and Economics 1983 *1* Autumn, pp 91–117
The case study discussed involved detailed evaluation of the defects; a pilot contract; a management contract approach; cost monitoring and performance monitoring; post contract cost control; innovative use of temporary shelters.

364
P. W. G. Morris
PROJECT MANAGEMENT ORGANISATION
Construction Papers 1983 *2* (1), pp 5–18
Current concepts of the organisation of large projects

are reviewed. The origins of project management are described and the essential patterns of organisation found on projects are detailed. In conclusion some practical lessons of project organisation are given, drawn from a variety of international projects.

363
J. Berny and R. Howes
PROJECT MANAGEMENT CONTROL USING REAL TIME BUDGETING AND FORECASTING MODELS
Construction Papers 1983 *2* (1), pp 19–40

362
G. Ridout
CONTRASTING BUILDING MENUS FAVOUR AFTER-TASTE AT TWO BOOT HOTELS
Contract Journal 1983 *316* December 15, pp 16–17
The progress is shown to be significantly different on two equal-sized hotels,l one on a traditional contract with a steel frame and the other a management contract with precast concrete.

361
H. Knoepfel
SYSTEMATIC PROJECT MANAGEMENT
International Journal of Project Management 1983 *1* November, pp 234–241
A set of conceptual models for the management of projects on the basis of the physical system of constructed facilities is presented. The purpose, structures, boundaries, environment and objectives of these models and some of the application procedures are discussed.

360
O. Hogberg and A. Adamsson
SCANDINAVIAN VIEW OF PROJECT MANAGEMENT
International Journal of Project Management 1983 *1* November, pp 216–219
The effects are discussed of cultural variations in project management. Based on the experiences of project organisations and project control systems, some concepts for management and control are presented. The importance of realistic forecasting is emphasised.

359
G. P. Gilbert
STYLES OF PROJECT MANAGEMENT
International Journal of Project Management 1983 *1* November, pp 189–193
The factors that a project manager needs to take into account are discussed and the case is made for a greater emphasis to be placed on leadership.

358
N. Davis
CONSULTANT QS AND PROJECT MANAGEMENT
Chartered Quantity Surveyor 1983 *6* November, pp 132–133
Guidance is given on the possible methods of remuneration for project management services.

357
B. Waters
BALANCED APPROACH
Building 1983 *265* November 4, 28–30
The design-build approach to the construction of a

speculative office block is outlined. It is claimed that the approach strikes the right balance between architectural and commercial pressures.

356
Southern Counties Joint Consultative Committee for Building
MANAGEMENT IN CONSTRUCTION
Proceedings of a meeting held on 26 October 1983. pp27
The management of building projects is considered from three viewpoints:
The traditional approach by R. Paul
Project management in practice by A. Massey
Management contracting and its variants by G. S. Rendall

355
R. Cecil
KEEP THE PROFESSIONALS
Building 1983 *265* August 19, p 25
The argument is challenged that building consultants should be subject to the same kind of contractual sanctions as builders.

354
N. Parkyn
MARKETING MANAGEMENT
Building 1983 *265* August 19, pp 29–31
BDP's philosophy in regard to its project management services is explored.

353
J. F. Woodward
PROJECT MANAGEMENT EDUCATION LEVELS OF UNDERSTANDING AND MISUNDERSTANDING
Project Management 1983 *1* August, pp 173–178
The teaching of project management both in-house and at academic establishments is reviewed.

352
CONSULTANTS ON THE LINE
Building 1983 *264* July 29, p 22
It is argued that the architect could help stem the tide towards non traditional forms of contracting by imposing some of the disciplines on himself that are accepted by the contractor. These could include the imposition of a design programme and a warranty of fitness for purpose.

351
C. Davies
STUDIO IN STORE
Building 1983 *264* June 3, pp 36–38
The construction of a TV studios conversion let on a management contract is briefly discussed.

350
C. Davies
ARCHITECTS WITH A PACKAGE DEAL
Building 1983 *264* May 20, pp 30–35
A. Epstein & Sons offer a package deal, the difference being that the firm is one of architects not a builder. The firm's basic approach and its application to Sainsbury's supermarket in Cromwell Road, London are described.

349
A. Ashworth
CONTRACTUAL METHODS USED IN THE CONSTRUCTION INDUSTRY
Building Trades Journal 1983 *185* May 12, pp 24, 29
An outline is given of the principles of management contracts, turnkey operations and serial contracts.

348
J. Franks
ASSESSING THE ALTERNATIVE SYSTEMS FOR MANAGING THE BUILDING PROCESS
Building Trades Journal 1983 *185* May 12, p 40
An assessment is made of traditional contracting, management fee and package deal.

347
R. Ormerod
SUCCESSFUL EXPERIMENT
Building 1983 *264* April 15, pp 34–37
MEPC's design-build office scheme carried out by Henry Boot is described, particular attention being given to the management aspects.

346
J. Bennett and R. Flanagan
MANAGEMENT OPTIONS
Building 1983 *264* April 8, pp 32–33
New forms of contracting are seen as being of advantage to the client. The background to these new forms is traced and an outline given of the principles of project management, design and construct and construction management (management contracting).

345
C. Davies
FASTBUILD SYSTEM
Building 1983 *264* April 1, pp 31–34
The management of a design build contract is outlined, particular attention being given to the role of the architect within the team. Lack of an adequate client's brief resulted in £100000 of additional work.

344
C. B. Tatum
ISSUES IN PROFESSIONAL CONSTRUCTION MANAGEMENT
ASCE Journal of Construction Engineering and Management 1983 *109* (1) March, pp 112–119
The use of professional construction management has increased rapidly since the introduction of this form of organisation in the early 1960's. Despite this widespread use questions concerning the scope, definition, and differences in implementation of this project delivery system remain. An ASCE technical committee has investigated these questions and disseminated information concerning professional construction management through technical sessions at ASCE meetings, published papers, and a speciality conference. This paper summarises the results of these activities and provides references of the literature available regarding the development and use of professional construction management.

343
A. C. Sidwell
EVALUATION OF MANAGEMENT CONTRACTING
Construction Management and Economics 1983 *1* Spring, pp 47–55
The paper discusses the main features of the system of management contracting which has developed in the UK in the last decade and evaluates these in relation to those elements of the building process thought to influence project success. Data from a number of case studies are examined to establish the time saved and other advantages of using this system.

342
J. Franks
CONSTRUCTING A BRIDGE BETWEEN CLIENT, ARCHITECT AND BUILDER
Building Trades Journal 1983 *185* February 10, pp 28–29
The concept of project management is discussed.

341
J. Franks
SEPARATE CONTRACTS SYSTEM
Building Trades Journal 1983 *185* January 27, pp 22–23
The separate contracts system is basically where the architect lets contracts to individual trades rather than to a general contractor. The advantages and limitations of such a system are discussed.

340
SPECIAL REPORT, PROJECT MANAGEMENT
Chartered Surveyor Weekly 1983 *2* January 13, pp 84–85, 87, 89, 93
The report includes a number of separate contributions including an outline of the RICS' project management diploma course; the role for chartered surveyors; computer aids; and the financial/time benefits.

339
J. Franks
USING THE DESIGN AND BUILD SYSTEM
Building Trades Journal 1983 *185* January 6, p 14

338
J. F. Woodward
PROJECT MANAGEMENT: OCCUPATION OR VOCATION?
Project Manager 1983 *2* January, pp 2–3

337
H. Darnell and M. W. Dale
TOTAL PROJECT MANAGEMENT: AN INTEGRATED APPROACH TO THE MANAGEMENT OF CAPITAL INVESTMENT PROJECTS IN INDUSTRY
1983 Asset Management Group (BIM) pp 43

336
J. McKinney
MANAGEMENT CONTRACTING
CIOB Occasional Paper No. 30, 1983. pp 14
An evaluation is made of management contracting based on a review of the existing literature. The case is argued for the management contractor to be selected from contracting rather than the design professions. Following an outline of the development and growth of management contracting, attention is given to its market and the question of accountability when used in the public sector. Some useful guidance is given on the selection and operational stages before the final section which sums up the advantages and limitations.

335
Construction Industry Research and Information Association
MANAGEMENT CONTRACTING
Report No. 100. 1983. pp 44
The use of management contracting in the UK construction industry, predominantly in the building, process plant and offshore sectors is described. A review of construction management in the USA is also included. Management contracting is becoming more popular but in the UK it is still in an evolutionary phase. The problems with management contracting are identified and areas where improvements in practice could be made are indicated. The report is based on visits to 52 firms and organisations, 39 in the UK and 13 in the USA. Thirteen case studies are included, illustrating a variety of approaches to the management of construction projects. Potential weaknesses are identified. Provided these are recognised it is concluded that the various forms of management contracting can offer viable and flexible contractual relationships for projects where time is important, especially where there is a likelihood of insufficient design information being available at the stage when a main construction contract would normally be let. They are also suitable where there is a need to co-ordinate a considerable number of construction contractors and suppliers. Management contracting offers potential for improved management of design and construction, particularly where a client has insufficient resources or expertise to concentrate on these crucial aspects of managing a project.

334
British Property Federation
MANUAL OF THE BPF SYSTEM FOR BUILDING DESIGN AND CONSTRUCTION
1983, pp 99
The system is geared to both conventional and non traditional methods of procurement and it acts as a guide to the formal and informal team relationships. The main management functions of controlling time, cost, standards and performance are handled by a Client's Representative. For pre-tender design and specifications a Design Leader is appointed but the contractor is also allocated a proportion of the design to facilitate buildability. The system is in five stages but is flexible, allowing clients to decide where the dividing line between stages should be drawn. An adjudicator is appointed to deal quickly with disputes.

333
Construction Industry Research and Information Association
CLIENT'S GUIDE TO TRADITIONAL CONTRACT BUILDING
1983, pp 12

1982

332
J. Franks
PACKAGE DEAL SYSTEM HAS ALL THE CLIENTS' BUILDING NEEDS
Building Trades Journal 1982 *184* December 2, pp 24, 28
The principles of the package deal are outlined.

331
J. Franks
MANAGEMENT FEE CONTRACTS AND TWO STAGE TENDER SYSTEMS
Building Trades Journal 1982 *184* November 18, pp 37, 39

330
D. Hammond
PROJECT MANAGEMENT WHAT'S IT ALL ABOUT?
Contract Journal 1982 *310* November 11, pp 34–35
The concept of project management is outlined.

329
J. Franks
TRADITIONAL SYSTEM OF MANAGING THE BUILDING PROCESS
Building Trades Journal 1982 *184* November 4, pp 50, 52

328
I. Atkinson
INDUSTRY PUTS FPL ON PROJECT MANAGEMENT MAP
Contract Journal 1982 *309* November 4, pp 14–16
The approach is outlined of Fairclough Projects Ltd to management contracting in the industrial sector.

327
H. S. Kaden
INTERNATIONAL CONTRACTING
Proceedings of the CIB W-65 mini-symposium. The problems of organisation and management of construction in developing countries and international contracting. November 1982. Istanbul, pp 3.1.1–3.1.12
Attention is given to the role of the World Bank's procurement choices for the client and the salient points to be considered by a contractor on seeking an overseas contract.

326
A. C. Sidwell
PROJECT MANAGEMENT CONSIDERATIONS FOR INTERNATIONAL CONTRACTING
Proceedings of the CIB W-65 mini-symposium. The problems of organisation and mangement of construction in developing countries and international contracting. November 1982. Istanbul. pp 111/1–1—1–14.
The major variables likely to be encountered with an international project are discussed in addition to the problems posed by social, cultural, political, economic and educational differences. A case study is presented to illustrate the cultural role that the project management team plays. In conclusion four principal characteristics are highlighted which are particularly demanding of the project manager if success is to be achieved.

325
B. Waters
CONTRACTUAL SYSTEMS COMPARED: TWO HAMPSHIRE SPORTS BUILDINGS
Architects Journal 1982 *176* October 20, pp 67–74
The two contractual arrangements examined are design and build, and a managing contract, i.e. one in which the contractor was able to compete for packages of work.

324
LUDER VIEW ON THE MANAGING ARCHITECT
Contract Journal 1982 *309* September 2, pp 10–12
The architects role in project management is explored.

323
P. Carolin
DESIGNING FOR BUILDABILITY
Architects Journal 1982 *176* August 11, pp 32–33, 38, 41
The organisation is described of a management contracting carried out by Wimpey for civic offices, emphasis being given to the architects' role.

322
I. Atkinson
CONTRACTOR BUILDS MANAGEMENT SERVICE FOUNDED ON TRUST
Contract Journal 1982 *307* June 24, pp 12–14
Higgs & Hills approach to management contracting is outlined.

321
BUILDING METHODS AND MANAGEMENT
Financial times Survey 1982. June 30, pp 8
Among the subjects covered are management contracting, brick and timber frame, steel framed construction and a design building contract for Findus' Newcastle Plant.

320
I. Atkinson
'MOTIVATE AND MANAGE' IS THE DAVID WOOLF STYLE
Contract Journal 1982 *307* May 13, pp 16–17
Woolf Project Management's approach to management contracting is discussed.

319
I. Atkinson
SMOOTHING THE PATH OF DEVELOPMENT
Contract Journal 1982 *307* May 6, pp 12–14
Trollope and Colls approach to management contracting is discussed.

318
P. Sharp
MANAGEMENT OR FEE OR BOTH?
Chartered Quantity Surveyor 1982 *4* May, pp 307–309
A review is made of the place for fee and management contracting.

317
G. Trickey and J. Sims
DOES THE CLIENT GET WHAT HE WANTS?
Quantity Surveyor 1982 *38* May, pp 86–88
A summary is given of two talks given at

the 1982 Building Industry Convention. Particular attention is devoted to the traditional methods of procurement and how those fail to meet the clients requirements.

316
LAING TEAM CONFIDENT OF RESTORING SUCCESS
Construction News 1982 April 15, pp 18–19
An interview with the Chief Executive of John Laing, Leslie Holliday, which covers the future of the Group, the approach to training, Super Homes development, and management contracting.

315
P. D. Titmus
DESIGN AND BUILD IN PRACTICE
Building Technology and Management 1982 *20* April, pp 9–12
The case for the design and build approach to contracting is discussed, it being argued that one of its most important characteristics is the increased willingness of parties to find rapid solutions to problems and to overcome difficulties. Responsibilities are clearly defined thereby leading to a minimum of misunderstanding.

314
A. L. Y. Lewis
RECRUITMENT OF PROJECT MANAGEMENT STAFF
Project Manager 1982 2 April, pp 15–17
Some information is given on job specification, responsibilities, conditions of employment and recruitment.

313
A. Walker
LINEAR RESPONSIBILITY ANALYSIS
Chartered Quantity Surveyor 1982 *4* March, pp 228–230
Linear responsibility analysis is a tool which project managers use to design an appropriate organisation structure at an early stage.

312
BUILDING EFFICIENTLY: HOW THE AMERICANS MANAGE IT
RIBA Journal 1982 *89* March, pp 32–33
Two articles explore project management and the advantages of the North American approach to contracting.

311
C. B. Tatum
PROFESSIONAL CM: THE ARCHITECT ENGINEER'S VIEWPOINT
ASCE Journal of the Construction Division 1982 *108* (CO1). March, pp 177–178 (Discussion).

310
H. S. Crowter
NEW JCT DESIGN/BUILD CONTRACT – 1981
Quantity Surveyor 1982 *38* March, pp 42–44
A commentary is provided on the major articles and conditions.

309
N. Barratt
MANAGEMENT CONTRACTING TO PROVE ITS WORTH AT HEATHROW'S NEW TERMINAL
New Civil Engineer 1982 February 25, pp 12–14
The background is outlined to the development, advantages and current use of management contracting. The British Airports Authority is to let the construction of terminal 4 as a management contract.

308
DIRECT AND DESIGN
Building 1982 *262* February 26, pp 24–25
A profile is given of the design/build organisation the JT Group.

307
H. S. Crowter
NEW JCT DESIGN/BUILD CONTRACT – 1981
Quantity Surveyor 1982 *38* February, pp 25–27
A commentary is provided on the new form as it relates to professional advisers, design liability and VAT.

306
F. C. Graves
QUANTITY SURVEYOR AND PROJECT MANAGEMENT
Quantity Surveyor 1982 *38* February, pp 28–32
The benefits of project management and the functions of the project manager are discussed.

305
B. Waters
CONVERSION ON THE FAST TRACK
Building 1982 *262* January 15, pp 24–26
The conversation of an hotel to offices is described briefly, attention being given to the contractual arrangements which involved a project management organisation which was involved at inception and dealt with the costing and advising on the programme implications of alternative designs. The project management organisation saw its role as client's agent with the client contracting with 40 contractors using a modified AIA contract.

304
D. Sudjic
RICHARD ROGERS LTD: FAST TRACKING IN WALES
RIBA Journal 1982 *89* January, pp 31–33, 36–37
The construction is described of a microchip factory built in just over 15 months using a management contractor.

303
Aqua Group
TENDERS AND CONTRACTS FOR BUILDING
1982. 2nd edition. Granada. pp 100
Forms of contractual arrangement are described.

302
B. McGhie
IMPLICATIONS OF PROJECT MANAGEMENT
Proceedings 3rd Bartlett Summer School. 1981. Production of the built environment. 1982. pp 3.1–3.9

301
Chartered Institute of Building
PROJECT MANAGEMENT IN BUILDING
1982. pp 36
Combines two previously published papers:
— Project management in building issued as Occasional Paper No. 20
— Education for project management in building.

300
K. F. Branu
PROJECT MANAGEMENT
Building Technologists 1981–82, *8*, pp 17–23
Attention is given to instructions; the design team; appointment of consultants; and client/project manager liaison.

1981

299
L. W. Murray et al
MARKETING CONSTRUCTION MANAGEMENT SERVICES
ASCE Journal of the Construction Division 1981 *107* December, pp 665–677
A survey of ninety-five construction management firms and two hundred and twenty-two construction management clients was undertaken to assess marketing practices and preferences. Forty-nine firms and forty-six clients responded to the survey. An analysis of the firm's responses indicated that the most important determinant of contract awards was the amount of general experience of the firm. Clients stressed the importance of the quality of services provided by the firm. Clients desired more information to assess the quality of the firm's proposed project manager. A marketing model is developed to assist construction management firms in positioning their marketing efforts. The model focuses upon the project manager, the project team, and requires that the firm include information to enable the clients to evaluate the firm's flexibility of their problem solutions to the clients' construction management problems.

298
PROJECT MANAGEMENT AND MANAGEMENT CONTRACTING THEIR FUTURE ROLE
Building Technology and Management 1981 *19* October, pp 11–12

297
N. Davis
PACKAGE DEAL SERVICE AND FEES
Chartered Quantity Surveyor 1981 *4* October, pp 60–61
The scope of quantity surveyor's services in relation to package deals is discussed and proposals are made on establishing fees for these services.

296
A. Yates
OLD RELATIONS IN NEW CLOTHES
Chartered Quantity Surveyor 1981 *4* October, pp 64
The principles of management fee contracts and their particular strengths are discussed.

295
Mr. Barnes
PROJECT MANAGEMENT BY MOTIVATION
Proc. PMI/Internet Joint Symposium 'The World of Project Management' Boston, USA. September 1981, pp 341–346
The motivation factors are examined which are in some of the main sectors of project management – client's decisions, design, contracts and construction.

294
R. M. Davis and H. G. Irwig
PROJECT MANAGEMENT SERVICES: EFFECTIVENESS IN BUILDING CONSTRUCTION
Proc. PMI/Internet Joint Symposium 'The World of Project Management' Boston, USA. September 1981, pp 318–330
The evolution of the need for project management is discussed and the nature of the project manager's responsibilities are reviewed.

293
L. W. Murray and H. T. Moody
PROJECT MANAGER IN MARKETING PROFESSIONAL SERVICES
Proc. PMI/Internet Joint Symposium 'The World of Project Management' Boston, USA. September 1981, pp 364–373
The role is discussed of project managers in the marketing strategy of firms selling professional services. Market surveys exploring this role for project management and for process engineering design and construction are examined.

292
E. G. Trimble
MOTIVATION OF CONTRACTORS IN MEDIUM TECHNOLOGY PROJECTS
Proc. PMI/Internet Joint Symposium 'The World of Project Management' Boston, USA. September 1981, pp 257–261
The incentive value of different types of contractual arrangements are outlined.

291
Junior Liaison Organisation
THOSE SUCCESSFUL PRACTICES. HOW DO THEY DO IT?
Conference held at St. Edmund Hall, Oxford, September 1981. pp 40
The only substantial summary is that of the paper by T. W. Fleming on management contracting. The points covered are the type of project, design involvement, time, sub-letting, work packages, value for money, cost control, incentive to the management contractor, fees and industrial relations.

290
D. Byron
ROLE OF THE ARCHITECT IN NEW FORMS OF CONTRACTING SERVICES
Building Technology and Management 1981 *19* July/August, pp 13–14
Particular attention is given to design-build projects.

289
H. G. Irwig, R. M. Davis
CONSTRUCTION MANAGEMENT SERVICES IN BUILDING CONSTRUCTION: USE AND EFFEC-TIVENESS IN THE USA
Proceedings of the CIB W–65 3rd Symposium on Organisation and Management of Construction. Dublin, July 1981. Volume 1. pp A.1.234–A.1.251
A nationwide survey of 200 repeat purchasers of commercial, industrial and institutional buildings in continental USA and Canada to evaluate the pattern of usage and the degree of effectiveness of professional construction management services is reported. Analysis of the data reveals that:
— the use of construction management services is associated with projects of high complexity and value and moderate budget constraints. These characteristics do not, however, appear to be relevant in influencing either the type of construction managers utilised or the conditions of engagement.
— Although a very wide range of functions were regarded as primary responsibility areas for construction managers, only those concerned with the scheduling of construction, the negotiation and management of construction contracts, and the provision of preliminary budgets and cost projections were functions in which construction managers were generally perceived as being helpful.

288
T. M. Lewis
THE ROLE OF THE PROFESSIONAL CON-STRUCTION MANAGER
Proceedings of the CIB W–65 3rd Symposium on Organisation and Management of Construction. Dublin, July 1981. Volume 11. pp C.2.228–C.2.238

287
R. Fish
TENDERING AND CONTRACT PROCEDURES
Chartered Quantity Surveyor 1981 *3* July, pp 388–389
Tendering practice for industrial engineering contracts is discussed, reference being made to documentation, type of contract, conditions, contractor selection, and tender appraisal.

286
J. M. Hutcheson
PROJECT MANAGEMENT ACROSS CULTURAL BARRIERS
Proceedings of the CIB W–65 3rd Symposium on Organisation and Management of Construction. Dublin. July 1981. Volume II. pp C.1.52–C.1.67
A series of case studies and first hand experiences in developing and undeveloped countries are outlined. An evaluation is made of the construction problems encountered in these case studies with a view to synthesising lessons for project management. Human relations, legal, financial and other aspects are contrasted with their relationships in project management in countries with different cultures. Studies of overheads encountered by consultants and constructors operating away from their homeland are highlighted.

285
P. T. Pigott
APPLICATION OF THE SfB SYSTEM TO PROJECT MANAGEMENT
Proceedings of the CIB W–65 3rd Symposium on Organisation and Management of Construction. Dublin. July 1981. Volume I. pp A.1.409–A.1.415

284
A. Walker
ANALYSING BUILDING PROJECT MANAGEMENT STRUCTURES
Project Manager 1981 *2* July, pp 6–11
A method (linear responsibility analysis) is described by which post-mortems can be carried out on building projects which allow the organisational causes of deficiencies in the outcome of projects to be identified.

283
G. Smith
TENDERING PROCEDURES SCRUTINISED. ESSEX COSTS THE ALTERNATIVES
Chartered Quantity Surveyor 1981 *11* June, pp 356–357
The cost effects of alternative tendering procedures, based on questionnaire and interview, are evaluated. Data are provided on the frequency of use of different procedures (competitive; negotiated; two-stage; cost plus fee; design and build), frequency of use of procedures for specialist works, average difference in pricing levels for main contract procedures, cost to client, total tendering costs, and average tenderer's costs for each from submitting a tender.

282
J. A. Ramsay
PROFESSIONAL CM: THE ARCHITECT: ENGI-NEERS VIEWPOINT
ASCE Journal of the Construction Division 1981 *107* June, pp 408–409 (Discussion)
Views supporting the project management concept are expressed.

281
P. W. T. Pippin
PROJECT MANAGEMENT. THE THIRD DISCIPLINE IN ARCHITECTURAL PRACTICE
Architectural Record 1981 June, pp 63, 65
It is argued that project management is of equal importance to design and production. The basic aims of a project manager and the advantages of project management are discussed.

280
V. Ireland
MODELLING THE BUILDING PROCESS. 4. SEQUENTIAL LUMP SUM TENDERING VERSUS PROJECT MANAGEMENT
Chartered Builder 1980/81 *31* Summer, pp 73, 75–78
A critique is made of general systems theory from which the action approach is stated and a model developed which can be applied to design, tendering and construction. A model representing project management is also developed.

279
DESIGN AND BUILD - THE QS OPPORTUNITY
Quantity Surveyor 1981 *37* aay, pp 95–96

278
D. Pritchard
QS VIEW OF MANAGEMENT CONTRACTING
Construction News Magazine 1981 7 May, pp 13–14
The advantages and limitations of management contracting are summarised, the type of project for which it is particularly suitable being identified.

277
TALKING THE CONTRACT THROUGH
Building 1981 *260* April 23, pp 28–30
A group discussion is reported on the building industry's ability to meet the client needs, the significance of contractual arrangements being paramount.

276
R. Mortimer
DESIGN AND CONSTRUCT, ITS GROWTH, SHORT-COMINGS ETC.
Paper to RICS Quantity Surveyor 12th Triennial Conference, April 1981, pp 5.

275
H. Davis
ADVANTAGES OF MANAGEMENT CONTRACTS APPARENT OR REAL?
Paper to RICS Quantity Surveyor 12th Triennial Conference, April 1981, pp 10
The basic principles of management contracting are considered, reference being made to some projects built using the arrangement. Disadvantages and advantages are indicated.

274
J. B. G. Carpenter
UK SYSTEM OF CONSTRUCTION PROCUREMENT AND WHAT IS WRONG HOW TO IMPROVE
Paper to RICS Quantity Surveyor 12th Triennial Conference, April 1981, pp 16
It is suggested that projects go wrong because the actual tasks peculiar to the project are not clearly identified. This failure prevents appropriate procedures being developed for the project. Particular attention is given to the roles, assumed and actual, of all participants to the building process.

273
A. Walker
MODEL FOR THE DESIGN OF PROJECT MANAGEMENT STRUCTURES
Quantity Surveyor 1981 *37* April, pp 66–71
The salient features of the model, the methodology and the results obtained are identified and discussed.

272
P. G. Cheesman
WHAT IS PROJECT MANAGEMENT AND WHO ARE PROJECT MANAGERS
Project Manager 1981 *2* April, pp 19–21
The scope of project management and the project manager's role are discussed – the functions of a project manager are given as an appendix.

271
J. F. Woodward
TRAINING FOR PROJECT MANAGEMENT
Project Manger 1981 *2* April, pp 17–19

270
T. Farrow
IN PLACE OF STRIFE
Building 1981 *260* March 27, p 47
An outline is given of the principles of project management.

269
R. Flanagan
CHANGE THE SYSTEM
Building 1981 *260* March 20, pp 28–29
Some of the arguments for non-traditional forms of letting contracts are presented.

268
A. P. Carpenter
DESIGN AND CONTRACT PROCEDURE COMPARISONS
Building Economist 1981 *19* March, pp 217–225
A review is made of the RICS report comparing the UK and US construction industries and at the same time a comparison is made of the selling price and achieved times of the Australian industry.

267
H. Schlick
PROFESSIONAL CM: THE ARCHITECT: ENGINEERS VIEWPOINT
ASCE Journal of the Construction Division 1981 *107* March, pp 158–159 (Discussion)

266
R. Moxley
DESIGN/SUPERVISE/BUILD
Architects Journal 1981 *173* February 25, pp 359–363
Practical application is demonstrated of the AMM approach to building in which the architect was involved on a day to day basis on site, and no midddleman main contractor was employed.

265
T. Frost
UNCONVENTIONAL ALTERNATIVES
Quantity Surveyor 1981 *37* February, pp 30–31
Some thoughts are expressed on the variety of contractual arrangements available to clients and on the value of the QS in giving appropriate advice.

264
Lam Cheok Weng
TURNKEY CONTRACT PROFESSIONAL VIEWS
Building Technologists 1981–82 *8,* pp 118–125
The views are expressed of Malaysian personnel.

263
Bovis Construction Ltd.
SELECTION OF A MANAGEMENT CONTRACTOR FOR THE PUBLIC SECTOR
1981. pp 13

262
CIRIA
CLIENT'S GUIDE TO DESIGN BUILD
1981. pp 12

261
G. Peters
PROJECT MANAGEMENT AND CONSTRUCTION CONTROL
1981. Construction Press. pp 131

Concerned primarily with client-orientated project management, chapters are included on contracts, decision making, programme planning, materials procurement, project control and monitoring and project estimating.

1980

260
I. Fraser
AMM CASE STUDY, DESIGNING AND BUILDING A PRIMARY SCHOOL
Architects Journal 1980 *172* December 10, pp 1163–1166
AMM (Alternative Methods of Management) has the architect as full time designer and project controller. With no general contractor the client employs specialist contractors and trades directly through the architect. The aims are speed and quality through rapid communication and close control of work. Aspects of the specific project discussed include the contractual approach, the role of the job architect, insurances, contracts, valuations, programming, tendering, and site works. Speed and quality were achieved. Areas requiring closer attention on subsequent jobs would include cost control, manpower planning and supervision levels.

259
J. Dressler
CONSTRUCTION MANAGEMENT IN WEST GERMANY
ASCE Journal of the Construction Division 1980 *106* December, pp 477–487
In Germany, both professional construction management and construction management techniques have been refined during the last two decades. Increasingly, modern management techniques to plan and control time, resources, and costs of construction processes are used by owners and by the construction industry. A brief overview is given on the status of the German construction industry within the German economy. Project management techniques commonly used in the country are reviewed. Emphasis is given to the velocity diagram. Construction management concepts are presented as used on several large construction projects in Germany. Differences with regard to various owners will be illustrated.

258
R. J. Christesen and C. B. Tatum
LABOUR RELATIONS CONSIDERATIONS ON PCM PROJECTS
ASCE Journal of the Construction Division 1980 *106* December, pp 535–549
Implementation of effective labour relations programmes is essential for successful professional construction management (PCM) projects. This paper identifies elements of such programmes and proposes responsibility assign

ment. Implementation tasks and actions to integrate the contractor programmes are also examined. To provide a background of relevant construction industry characteristics, an overview of industry scope and organisation is presented. Specific objectives are then defined for labour relation programmes on PCM projects. Tasks and method of implementation, including both the initial project programme and those of each specific contractor are examined. Suggestions are also included for avoiding common problem areas by anticipation and early resolution. To further highlight the unique requirements of labour relations programmes on PCM projects, essential differences from other forms of organisation are reviewed.

257
H. I. Davis
SDADVANTAGES OF DESIGN AND BUILD TO THE PRIVATE EMPLOYER
Paper to Company Communications Centre Seminar, 'Joint Ventures', London, 25–26 September 1980, pp 15 (Summary)
In discussing the advantages of design and build contracts reference is made to risk, conflict of interest and communication and responsibility. Examples are given to illustrate the cost benefits of the approach.

256
D. A. Macniven
MONITORING A MANAGEMENT CONTRACT
Chartered Quantity Surveyor 1980 *3* September, pp 52–53
Brief details are given of a quantity surveyor's experience of a management contract. Difficulties associated with the number of sub-contractors and associated delays are mentioned. The major benefit resulting from the use of a management contract was that design time available was maximised by the programming of work packages and obtaining competitive tenders for each of the sections of the work.

255
D. S. Barris
GUIDELINES FOR SUCCESSFUL CONSTRUCTION MANAGEMENT
ASCE Journal of the Construction Division 1980 *106* (CO3) September, pp 237–245
Some of the somewhat controversial and undefined areas of the professional construction management approach are reviewed. The discussion and suggested guidelines include the assignment of liabilities and risk, labour relations considerations, compensation and fee structures, forms of contract, organisational concepts and licensing considerations. A discussion of the responsibilities and qualifications of each of the team members (designer, owner, and construction manager) is included. To be successful, the three-party team must have the proper individual qualifications and each team member must respect and appreciate the skills and professionalism of the other.

254
B. C. Paulson Jr. and A. Tsuneo
CONSTRUCTION MANAGEMENT IN JAPAN
ASCE Journal of the Construction Division 1980 *106* (CO3) September, pp 281–196
Components of the industry that are described include public works agencies, trade and professional associations, approximately half a million contractors, private owners, banking, and trading groups. Other sections of the paper give more detail on ranking and prequalification of

contractors by public and private owners, selection of bidders, factors affecting project design and construction, project management, specialty contractors, and methods and techniques for project control. Although many factors would ease acceptance of professional construction management approach, three potential obstacles include: (1) Close interdependencies between general contractors and their subcontractors; (2) ambiguities in contract administration related to 'Confucian sense of social obligation'; and (3) legal restrictions preventing commencement of projects before all plans and specifications have been completed and approved by building officials. Nevertheless, there is strong interest in adapting this method to Japanese conditions.

253

A. Heaphy

CONTRACTS IN THE USA

Building Technology and Management 1980 *18* July/August, pp 29–32

Following a short assessment of the development of the US construction industry and current developments, attention is given to contractual arrangements. Reference is made to lump sum, cost plus, guaranteed maximum, design-build, and construction management contracts. Services offered by the contractor under the latter contract are described in some detail.

252

J. L. Lammie and D. P. Shah

PROJECT MANAGEMENT – PULLING IT ALL TOGETHER

ASCE Transportation Engineering Journal 1980 *106* July. pp 437–451

New innovative managerial techniques employed in a US Rapid Transit Authority allowing control and co-ordination during the first phase of the project are discussed.

251

S. B. Tietz

WHEN TIME IS OF THE ESSENCE . . .

Structural Engineer 1980 *58A* July, pp 225–228 (Discussion)

The discussion relates to reducing the time to get the design to tender stage, reference being made to package deals and management contracts.

250

F. Perryman

DEFINING THE ROLES OF THE DESIGN ENGINEER AND CONTRACTOR, PART 2

QS Weekly 1980 June 26, pp 8–9

Methods of tendering are indicated that are particularly applicable to designers, contractors. Responsibilities in relation to co-ordination are considered before attention is given to pre– and post-tender cost control.

249

N. Heayes

MANAGEMENT CONTRACTING SURGES FORWARD

Contract Journal 1980 *295* June 26, pp 21–23

An overview is given of the current status of project management, some of its advantages and the scope of its application being discussed by practitioners.

248

C. B. Tatum et al

PROFESSIONAL CM: THE ARCHITECT/ENGINEER'S VIEWPOINT

ASCE Journal of the Construction Division 1980 *106* June, pp 141–153

The professional construction management form of organisation is gaining increased usage because of distinct advantages offered on certain types of projects. The paper examines the viewpoint of the architect/engineer (A/E) serving as a member of the CM team under this delivery system. The role of the A/E, including differences in A/E performance as contrasted with the traditional form of project organisation, is considered in detail Key A/E tasks during each phase of the project are identified. Elements of effective A/E performance, including responsiveness, responsibility, field organisation, and design documents are analysed. The writers conclude that the potential benefits of this project delivery system can be best realised by a precise definition of the A/E role. The A/E must be both aware of differences in performance under this system and receptive to construction input from the CM. Practical application of the concepts presented from the A/E viewpoint lies in avoidance of common problems on CM projects and the full support of the PCM team.

247

M. Spring

PACKAGED WITH DESIGN

Building 1980 *238* May 23, pp 28–30

The factors leading to a medium sized industrial client choosing a package deal for its new factory are identified. Consultant quantity surveyors were asked to compile a draft building specification and to assist in selecting the contractor. Advantages of the approach as they were found in practice are outlined.

246

F. A. Hammond

CONTRACTUAL SYSTEMS

Paper to CICC Conference, 'Financial policy and control in construction projects' London. 15/16 May 1980. pp 25–35.

Some thoughts are expressed on the role the client should play in determining his requirements and in selecting the contractual arrangement best suited to his purpose. This is followed by a summary of the basic principles of the design and build, traditional, management contracting, and project management approaches to letting a contract.

245

M. Snowdon

PROJECT MANAGEMENT

ICE Proc. 1980 *68* Part 1, May, pp 309–312

244

J. Wesselman et al

MANAGING SUPER PROJECTS IN THE PUBLIC SECTOR: THE PUBLIC AGENCY CONSULTANCY

Paper to ASCE Annual Convention. Portland, April 14–18, 1980. pp 16

Programme management is where the public agency delegates the authority for management and technical services to contractors who then operate under close monitoring by agency personnel. The advantages of this approach are described with reference to client and consultant relations, relations with receiving agencies, relations with the public, and efficiency and cost effectiveness.

243
G. M. Gans
CONSTRUCTION MANAGER AND SAFETY
Paper to ASCE Annual Convention, Portland April 14–18, 1980. pp 18
A variety of approaches to safety are described for application with the professional construction management system. Some of the current problems in performance, legality and regulatory interpretation which accompany these approaches are discussed.

242
T. Frost
AND NOW FOR SOMETHING COMPLETELY DIFFERENT
Quantity Surveyor 1980 *36* April, pp 62–64
the experiences reported of a QS acting as project manager for the construction of a Chaplaincy Centre for the campus of Bristol Polytechnic. The role was to organise and co-ordinate the construction, to liaise with the Manpower Services Commission (grant provider) and other external organisations, and to provide regular cost and progress information to the trustees.

241
R. Winsor
IS GOD A PROJECT MANAGER?
Project Manager 1980 *2* April, pp 16–17
An architect identifies four principles of good project management as being a clear objective, a plan of action, healthy relationships, and effective communication.

240
P. Taylor and P. Cox
GETTING A BUILDING BUILT
Chartered Builder 1980 *29* April, pp 29–31
Basic procedures for a number of methods of tendering are outlined. These include selective and negotiated tendering, open selected tendering, management contracting, and fixed fee tendering.

239
F. Wai
PROJECT MANAGEMENT IN HONG KONG
Quantity Surveyor 1980 *36* February, pp 20–22
The role of the project manager is described, and the advantages discussed of employing this approach.

238
M. Snowden
PROJECT MANAGEMENT
Quantity Surveyor 1980 *36* January, pp 2–4
A background is given to the understanding of project management. It is seen as a series of the following ten steps. Establish the background to the project; define the objectives; determine the criteria for success; draw up an action plan; establish base for control; mobilise resources; set up required organisation; monitor progress, control and set to work.

237
Bovis Construction Ltd.
"BUILDING BUSINESS. THE CLIENT'S GUIDE TO CONSTRUCTION"
1980, pp 14
Details are given of the fee and management type

contracts operated by the company, the advantages to the client being identified.

1979

236
C. J. Liddle and A. J. Wallace
PROJECT MANAGEMENT OF CONSTRUCTION WITH RESPECT TO PROCESS INDUSTRIES AT HOME AND ABROAD
Structural Engineer 1979 *57A* December, pp 401–406
A comparison is made of project management at home and abroad. After describing the growth of consultancy in the process industries, culminating in the multi-discipline management consultant, the point is made that, for major industrial projects, the process engineer fulfils the function that the architect contributes to home-based building projects. The accepted duties of project management are then described.

235
J. W. Rogers
PROJECT MANAGEMENT A MANAGING CONTRACTOR'S APPROACH
Structural Engineer 1979 *57A* December, pp 407–409
A managing contractor's (Taylor Woodrow) approaches to project management in the UK is described. The importance of the role of the client is emphasised and the general functions and sequence of operations of the project manager are identified. Co-ordination of design disciplines for multi-discipline projects is stressed, together with the need for an effective system for the control of changes or modifications. It is suggested that the contractor is ideally suited to develop a project management capability. Finally, five factors are listed which are considered essential to a satisfactory outcome to the services provided.

234
D. J. Dickinson
PROJECT MANAGEMENT THE CLIENT'S VIEW
Structural Engineer 1979 *57A* December, pp 410–414
The role of the client is discussed in the management of his own projects. The terms of engagement of a professional services are considered and some of the ways are discussed by which the written word of the contracts is no longer adequate. An 'in-house' set of conditions of control is referred to which places more responsibility on the client and the contractor than on the team of professionals. The relative success of this approach over 10 years is discussed.

233
D. S. Barrie
TRADE CONTRACTORS' VIEW OF CONSTRUCTION
ASCE Journal of the Construction Division 1979 *105* (CO4) December, pp 381–387
Conclusions are reached through the use of questionnaires obtained from contractors who have performed on construction management projects. A tabulation of the results shows the comments about the projects surveyed were favourable from the speciality contractors. Less favourable comments were received about design changes or modifications made after award of the contract. Following a work plan, awarding contracts in an

ethical manner and prequalifying contractors is necessary for a successful project.

232

K. A. Kettle

PROPOSED CONSTRUCTION MANAGEMENT

ASCE Journal of the Construction Division 1979 *105* (CO4) December, pp 367–380

A specification is presented for use in Agreements for construction management services. Precise wording is used throughout, and definitions provided for words that might result in variable interpretations. A cover sheet provides a brief review of the use of the specification together with necessary inclusions in the Agreement between the Owner and the Construction Manager.

231

A. C. Paterson

IMPORTANCE OF PROJECT MANAGEMENT

Structural Engineer 1979 *57A* December, pp 399–400

An overview is given of the role of British consultants acting as project managers overseas.

230

N. Evans

ON SITE MANAGEMENT TODAY

Paper to Interbuild Seminar, Birmingham, 5 December 1979, pp 4

Consideration is given to management contracting, i.e. the organisation of construction by selected sub-contractors, reference being made to the services involved, and the operation of a management contract.

229

PETER TROLLOPE PUTS UP A SOUND CASE FOR PROJECT MANAGEMENT

Construction News 1979 November 1, p 19

The case for project management is argued and is maintained that it is in the areas of overall performance – time, budget and quality – that project management will make its biggest contribution. It will provide the overall co-ordination and control of the project in the pre-contract and construction stages, bringing clarity of thought and discipline to decision making.

228

G. Goulden

BUILDING ON DESIGN

Building 1979 *237* November 16, pp 36–37

The structure and operation are described of the Shepherd Design Group which offers a comprehensive design and build service.

227

A. Walker

APPROACH JTO THE DESIGN OF PROJECT MAN-AGEMENT STRUCTURES

Quantity Surveyor 1979 *35* October, pp 537–539

The potential is considered of thinking about construction projects in systems terms and the significance is discussed of the contingency theory in the understanding of project management.

226

H. R. Beaton

PROJECT CONTROLS MANUAL v MACHINE

Paper to ASCE Convention, Atlanta, October 22–26, 1979, pp 14

Systems available to the project manager to assist in the initiation, management and completion of a project are discussed in relation to the five major phases of the project – project definition; engineering and design, procurement; construction; project management. Two areas are examined where the project manager does not receive significant support from the computer – financial and timing controls.

225

E. B. Smith and M. F. Fishette

CONSTRUCTION MANAGEMENT IN THE MIDDLE EAST

Paper to ASCE Convention, Atlanta, October 23–25, 1979, pp 22

The basic components of project management and the particular requirements of Saudi Arabia are discussed. Potential problem areas such as logistics, project mobilisation, communications, and local customs, are identified.

224

J. Hinckley

LESSER DESIGN AND BUILD MORE A WAY OF STRIFE

QS Weekly 1979 October 4, pp 8–9

An interview is reported with Harvey David, MD of Lesser Design and build, which considers the advantages of the design and build approach and its future prospects.

223

C. B. Tatum

EVALUATING PCM FIRM POTENTIAL AND PER-FORMANCE

ASCE Journal of the Construction Division 1979 *105* September, pp 239–251

A set of criteria for evaluating the portential and performance of professional construction management (PCM) firms is proposed. Based on the work of the ASCE Committee on PCM, these criteria relate to a task list of PCM services. The criteria, both subjective and objective, cover each of the five phases of most construction projects. Following suggestion of criteria, a methodology for PCM evaluation is presented. This methodology includes defining the extent of evaluation required, obtaining the necessary information, and performing the evaluation. Both selection of a PCM firm for a future project and evaluating a PCM on an active project are addressed. Practical application of the criteria defined, in both selection and evaluation is reviewed.

222

J. D. Madsen

PROFESSIONAL CONSTRUCTION MANAGEMENT SERVICES

ASCE Journal of the Construction Division 1979 *105* June, pp 139–156

A full range of professional construction management (PCM) tasks are identified that may be utilised on major construction projects. This listing is based on the work of the ASCE committee on PCM. Identification of the essential tasks of a professional construction manager, as a basis for measuring performance, was the primary purpose of this work. Basic attributes of an effective PCM firm are presented. The functional PCM tasks are divided into the five phases of major construction projects; (1) conceptual planning; (2) program planning; (3) design construction; (4) close-out; and (5) start up. For each of these phases, the primary PCM services and tasks are identified. Examples are included where appropriate. Practical application for selection of a firm, evaluation of a firm on an active project, or self-auditing by a PCM firm, is discussed. The successful PCM firm must be multi-disciplinary, include all control functions, and provide a broad spectrum of management, engineering, construction, systems and legal expertise.

221
C. Reed
CM IN FEDERAL BUILDING CONSTRUCTION
Constructor 1979 *41* June, pp 33–35
An outline is given of how construction (project) management is used by federal building agencies in the US. Reservations are expressed of the practice where the architect retained to design a project also acts as construction manager.

220
R. P. Maher
COMPLEX PROBLEMS WITH SEPARATE CONTRACTS SYSTEM
ASCE Journal of the Construction Division 1979 *105* June, pp 129–137
Contracting systems used in the construction industry today are presenting new and complex problems and those engaged in the industry should be aware of them. The construction management concept used to produce construction today has adapted the separate contract system to implement its purpose. The concept, which itself is relatively new, is adapting an old system in different ways without looking to the legal, technical, and management problems involved. It is using these systems in a number and at a rate at which the slower processes of law cannot keep pace with. Three major problems are presented here. They are not solved because the solutions wait on the law. The purpose of this paper is to hopefully serve as a signal or reminder to the industry and to bring to the industry's notice some of these problems in the hope that its members will recognise them and act accordingly.

219
RIGHT FORM OF DESIGN AND CONSTRUCT?
Contract Journal 1979 *239* June 21, pp 25–27
A discussion with the deputy executive of the IDC Group is reported which covers the need for a contract for package deal contracts, particularly for industrial buildings.

218
M. Barnes
GROWTH OF INDEPENDENT PROJECT MANAGEMENT.
Proc. Company Communications Centre Seminar. 'Tendering and Contracting in the UK', London, April 1979, pp 25–29
Brief consideration is given to the skills and attitude of the project manager and the project manager's contract.

217
G. C. Trickey
PROCEDURES FOR TENDERING AND CONTRACTING
Proc. Company Communications Centre Seminar. 'Tendering and Contracting in the UK', London, April 1979, pp 14–24
The development of the design and build method of contracting is discussed and compared with the traditional approach. Minimum ingredients to be contained within a design and build contract are identified and some guidelines are presented on tenders and tender evaluation. Finally, consideration is given to contractual responsibilities.

216
G. H. Brown
CASE STUDIES OF INTERNATIONAL TENDERING METHODS AND FORM OF CONSTRUCTION CONTRACTS
Paper to CICC Easter Conference 1979 'International Construction', University of NOttingham, April 5 and 6, pp 53–57
A form of contract is described for a design and build project in Saudi Arabia involving the construction of 1664 flats in 32 high rise towers. A comparison is made with the FIDIC form of contract.

215
R. Penwarden
OVERSEAS PROJECT MANAGEMENT
Paper to CICC Easter Conference 1979 'International Construction', University of Nottingham, April 5 and 6, pp 111–123
The organisation necessary to execute the works following the award of an overseas design and construct contract is described. The various head office organisational functions and controls are set out which are employed in co-ordinating the design, materials procurement, subcontractors work, and the roles and functions of the construction organisation carrying out the works.

214
D. S. Barrie
TRADE CONTRACTOR'S VIEW OF CONSTRUCTION MANAGEMENT
Paper to ASCE Convention and Exposition, Boston, USA, April 2–6 1979, pp 11
An assessment is made, from the specialist subcontractor's viewpoint, of project management. It is concluded that design changes after award cause most of the major problems in construction; responsibilities should be closely defined; contracts co-ordinated by the owner directly must be fully integrated into the programme so that interfaces can be both described in tender documents and co-ordinated during construction; information must pass through the project manager.

213
D. B. Neff
OWNER'S VIEW OF OVERCOMING PROJECT PROBLEMS
Paper to ASCE Convention and Exposition, Boston, USA, April 2–6 1979, pp 18
Following an outline of the difficulties faced by an owner in getting a building built, consideration is given to types of client, the six main phases of a project, and the various

contractual arrangements available, the advantages and disadvantages of each being indicated. The value of project management is discussed and the role and functions of a project manager are described.

212
C. Popescu
PITFALLS OF GSA-CMCS SOFTWARE
ASCE Journal of the Construction Division 1979 *105* (CO1) March, pp 95–106
General Service Administration had implemented a phase construction management approach for new Federal construction. PHase construction involves the overlapping of design and construction activities in a carefully planned, executed, and controlled order. In response to the above change, GSA adopted a modified IBM-CPM package. The system itself is made up of modules or groups of reports that are structured by type of information and by management level. As a result of information at two universities, pitfalls of this GSA-CMCS are presented. At the present time, the construction industry is in need of a good CPM project management and control system accessible to all contractors and educators at a low cost – GSA-CMCS does not fulfill this general requirement at the present stage.

211
P. E. Emmett
ALTERNATIVE METHODS OF MANAGEMENT. PROGRAMMING: RESPONSIBILITIES AND TECHNIQUE
Chartered Quantity Surveyor 1979 *1* February, pp 52–53
AMM is a form of project management in which the architect and QS retain their traditional relationships with the client and work through a main contractor, or preferably with a number of specialist contractors. It facilitates communication and gives better control of quality, cost and time. The system of estimating and programming adopted by AMM – based on statistical information and the cost/time method of estimating – is described.

210
MANAGEMENT CONTRACTING: HENRY BOOT'S NEW APPROACH
Construction News 1979 January 18, pp 14–15
An interview with David Woolf, managing director of Henry Boot Construction discusses the company's approach to management contracting with particular attention to client satisfaction, time, types of suitable job, cost savings, sub-contractors and possible developments.

209
Associated General Contractors of America
"OWNER'S GUIDE: BUILDING CONSTRUCTION CONTRACTING METHODS"
pp 11
An outline is given of contractual arrangements, including lump sum contracts, cost plus contracts, guaranteed maximum or upset price contracts, construction management contracts, design build contracts and turnkey contracts.

208
PROJECT MANAGEMENT IN ACTION
Chartered Builder 1979 *26,* pp 65–68
An outline is given of the construction of a hospital in Queensland. The project management system employed allowed the design to be developed to a stage where detail adequate for competitive tendering was attained. At this point design was frozen. In this way design and construction develop progressively so that the basic building components are constructed parallel to design and development of later components.

207
M. Snowdon
PROJECT MANAGEMENT
ICE Proc 1979 *66* (Part 1), pp 625–633
Based on the concept of a capital project being an instrument of change, the management steps of a project are analysed and shown to be wider than is commonly supposed. Because of this perspective it is possible to emphasise the early stages of activity and the sponsor's role throughout. As well as retaining normally available design and construction resources, the sponsor has to ensure that management resources are adequate, project manager selection and training are touched upon.

1978

206
P. F. Rad and M. C. Miller
TRENDS IN USE OF CONSTRUCTION MANAGEMENT
ASCE Journal of the Construction Division 1978 *104* (CO4) December, pp 515–523
Construction management generally refers to a contractual relationship whereby an owner secures professional management services of a large multi-discipline firm for a specific construction project. This newly found market for construction management services has created a proliferation of designer, constructor, and management firms competing for construction-management contracts, each offering their own version of construction–management services. An analysis of the data provided in the top contractor and designer firm listings for the past six years showed that the use of construction management grew throughout the design-construct industry by 9% between 1971 and 1976. Currently, 50% of the design firms are more likely to offer construction-management services as well. Larger firms are more likely to offer construction-management services although this service is more common to the engineer-architect design firms.

205
L. Clements
KESSOCK BRIDGE DESIGN AND BUILD CONTRACT PROCEDURES
Structural Engineer 1978 *56A* December, pp 345–346; Discussion 1980 *58* February, pp 52–58
The requirements are determined for design and build tendering and the procedures associated with them are identified. the discussion includes contributions from unsuccessful tenderers.

204

G. Suhanic

PROJECT MANAGER CAN DELIVER HIS CAPITAL COST PROJECT IN 16 WAYS

Trans. 5th Int. Cost Engineering Congress, Utrecht, October/November 1978, pp 158–163

Sixteen different ways by which a client may procure a building from lump sum, design/build to lease/purchase – are delineated and defined in relation to each other and the client. An indication is given of the role of the cost engineer.

203

C. O. Bonar

EFFECTIVE TOOLS FOR PROJECT MANAGERS

Trans. 5th Int. Cost Engineering Congress, Utrecht, October/November 1978, pp 199–206

The increasing relevance of project management is discussed before consideration is given to the essential activities in the areas of risk assessment; organisation structuring and project responsibility definition; application of selective controls based on risk assessment; control of changes to scope, contracts and responsibilities; and the control and use of management reserves.

202

D. N. Mitten

CONSTRUCTION MANAGEMENT ON COMPLETED PROJECTS OF THE GSA IN CONTRAST WITH TRADITIONAL CONTRACTING

Trans. 5th Int. Cost engineering Congress, Utrecht, October/November 1978, pp 85–93

A comparison made on five specific projects of the actual design and construction time using construction management (CM) and similar projects using traditional methods. It was found that CM was a superior organising and controlling technique and that GSA realised savings of 23.1% of construction cost when using CM combined with phased construction.

201

K. Brown

HALF-CENTURY OF BOVIS FEE

Construction News Magazine 1978 *4* October, pp 38–39, 41–43, 53–55

The development is traced of Bovis Construction with particular reference to its fee system. Mention is made of the close association with Marks and Spencer and details are given of some other contracts let under this system.

200

K. A. Godfrey Jnr.

PROFILE OF THE DESIGN/CONSTRUCTION COMPANIES

Civil Engineering 1978 *47* October, pp 131–136

An outline is given of the development of design/construct, particular reference being given to the approach by such as Koppers Co., Fluor and Ebasco Services.

199

B. J. Peachey

CONSTRUCTION PROJECT CONTROL

Paper to RICS Annual Conference, Harrogate, 26–29 September 1978, pp 18

The functions are described of the project manager (controller) reference being made to agreeing objectives, selection of the professional team, briefing, programme compilation, and the design solution. Contractual management, is then considered due regard being paid to contractor selection, communication and programming. A project management organisation diagram is presented as an appendix.

198

R. Porter

DESIGN/BUILD NEEDS CAREFUL THOUGHT AND PREPARATION

National Builder 1978 *59* September, p 322

The design/build concept is considered in relation to the requirements of the contractor, legal requirements and the developing market.

197

H. I. Davis

BOVIS METHODS OF CONTRACTING

Paper to DHSS Regional Quantity Surveyors Association Conference 'Alternative contractual methods', Newcastle-upon-Tyne, 22 June 1978, pp 14

An outline is given of the Bovis fee system, its advantages being highlighted and some examples of its use indicated.

196

S. J. Jenkins

DEVELOP AND CONSTRUCT CONTRACTING

Paper to DHSS REgional Quantity Surveyors Association Conference 'Alternative contractual methods', Newcastle-upon-tyne, 22 June 1978, pp 7

Following an outline of the background to develop and construct, the technique as currently applied is described. The design team take all decisions regarding site layout and development and produce the specification based mainly on performance requirements. The contractor is selected on single stage tendering with BOQ for site development and externals and the contractors firm price for each type of dwelling for super-structures and the price per block for substructures. The successful tenderer develops his design in collaboration with the design team.

195

K. Thain

CONSTRUCTION PROGRAMME MANAGEMENT

Paper to DHSS Regional Quantity Surveyors Association Conference 'Alternative contractual methods', Newcastle-upon-Tyne, 22 June 1978, pp 20

The project management service offered by Heery-Farrow is described, its advantages and limitations to the client being identified. Particular attention is given to the development of a compatible brief, contracting for design services, time/cost control, reporting and the on site management team.

194

J. Christopher

ARCHITECTURE OR BUSINESS

Building Design 1978 May 12, p 2

The advantages of the 'design and build' approach to contracting are assessed from which it is concluded that it has its place but not at the expense of the practice committed primarily to architecture.

193
P. Lord-Smith
PACKAGE-DEAL CONTRACTS
Architects Journal 1978 *167* May 3, pp 838–389 (Correspondence)
Reference is made to two new RIB (JCT) 'package deal' contracts and to the accompanying Practice Notes. The implications of the RIBA giving its approval to this form of contract are discussed.

192
I. Peters
PROJECTING THE QS AS MANAGER
Building 1978 *234* April 14, pp 73–74
The functions of the project manager are described, and the qualities and training of the QS which suit this role being identified.

191
D. Stephenson
MANAGEMENT CONTRACTING OVERSEAS THE PROBLEMS TO BE FACED
Construction News 1978 April 27, p 22
A report of a conference organised by the Export Group for the Constructional Industries covers the concept of project management, responsibilities, fee arrangements and selection.

190
R. Saville
SURVEYING THE FUTURE
Building 1978 *235* April 14, pp 67–68
An interview with the President of the RICS QS Division, David Male, is reported. It covers such topics as advertising, merger with the IQS, education and project management.

189
J. B. G. Carpenter
CLIENT'S VIEW OF THE CONSTRUCTION PROJECT MANAGER
Paper to RICS, Chartered Quantity Surveyor 11th Triennial Conference, London April 1978, pp 5
Consideration is given to the scale or type of project where a project manager is needed, the client's requirements, the responsibilities of the project manager, and the suitability of quantity surveyors for this role.

188
D. Johnston
IMPROVE YOUR RISK MANAGEMENT AVOID DESIGN LIABILITY
Constructor 1978 *60* April, pp 24–26
Some means are discussed by which US develop and construct or construction management contractors are attempting to reduce excessive liability for design faults.

187
B. J. Hill
DESIGN AND CONSTRUCT A CASE STUDY
Paper to RICS, Chartered Quantity Surveyors 11th Triennial Conference, London, April 1978, pp 15
A commentary is given on a major government contract for services accommodation where the builder was responsible for the provision of all working drawings from the client's original design drawings and specification. The contractor then had to build the project to a pre-determined budget to which he was already committed. The apparent advantages gained by the client, builder, consultants and specialist sub-contractors are discussed in full before consideration is given to ongoing management and financial controls.

186
C. Davies
PACKAGE DEAL POST OFFICE
Architect 1978 *124* March, pp 37–40
An architectural appraisal is made of the Liverpool central Post Office constructed by a package dealer. The involvement of design consultants is indicated.

185
W. Turner
DESIGN AND TENDER PROJECTS
Heating and Ventilating Engineer 1978 *52* March, pp 12–13
The implications of a contractor being invited to design and tender for the services of a building are considered from the contractor's and client's viewpoint. Limitations to the procedure are identified and some suggestions made whereby they can be avoided.

184
H. Dawson
MANAGEMENT CONTRACTING PRINCIPLES OF OPERATION IN SAUDI ARABIA
Middle East Construction 1978 *3* March, pp 78–79

183
FUTURE DEVELOPMENT THE CLIENT'S DILEMMA. PART 2
Quantity Surveyor 1978 *34* March, pp 112–121
A report is given of a conference, detailed summaries being provided of the following papers:
Commercial client's aims and experience by W. J. Mackenzie which discusses the client's philosophy in relation to his projected building, the client's role, and improvements required in regard to administration, time and workmanship. Public sector client's aims and experience by J. Boyce which considers procurement – serial tendering and design – build, consortia, efficiency of the industry, and professional services.
Part performance of the industry and the need for change by R. Warren-Evans which deals with the standard form of contract in relation to defects, professional fees and integrated design and payment systems.

182
E. Reid
JOB MANAGEMENT: AN ALTERNATIVE METHOD
Architects Journal 1978 *167* February 22, pp 355–357
the alternative method of management (AMM) evaluated has two fundamentals; it gets the architect back full time on site as the designer and project controller and it allows the various specialist contractors and trades to be employed by the client directly through the architect. It is concluded that AMM is suited mainly to projects over £350,000 and to rehab projects. It does enable projects to be completed faster than average and gives a close control on cost.

181
FUTURE DEVELOPMENT THE CLIENT'S DILEMMA. PART 1
Quantity Surveyor 1978 *34* February, pp 87–96
The aim of the conference reported was to examine the construction market from the viewpoint of both client and industry; to investigate the different forms of contract procurement, assess their performance, and provide a basis for discussion whilst at the same time clarifying the client's criteria and constraints. Individual contributions are given by R. Warren-Evans on the client's needs, by O. Luder on the architects' role, by F. Smith on the QS's role and by L. P. Whiting on the package deal.

180
J. Franks
PROJECT MANAGEMENT 10 ORGANISATIONS, PROFESSIONAL BACKGROUND AND TRAINING
Building Trades Journal 1978 *175* February 3, pp 12, 14–16, 18, 23
An outline is given of non-conventional methods of tendering including the package deal, a turnkey contracts, management contracting, design and construct and of the functions and responsibilities expected of the project manager – including contributions taken from the literature. Finally, consideration is given to existing facilities for the training of project management.

179
ALTERNATIVE METHOD OF MANAGEMENT
Building 1978 *234* January 27, pp 67, 69–70
A live case history of the use of the Alternative Method of Management (AMM) has been carried out by BRE. Applied to a rehabilitation job, it was chosen primarily because of the need to meet a tight time schedule. AMM involves the setting up of an office on site where the architect/manager who is to run the project resides full time, and the overlapping of the many activities as possible. The performance of AMM is evaluated, from which it is concluded that speed and quality control are achieved without reduction in standards.

178
ARCHITECT AND PROJECT MANAGEMENT
Building 1978 *234* January 27, pp 72–74
A discussion is presented on the AMM approach to project management. Educationalists regarded it as one of a number of possible alternative approaches which must be reflected in any educational approach. Nevertheless, there was research backing for the effectiveness of this system of project management by architects.

177
DESIGN/BUILD. A DIFFERENT SOLUTION?
Building 1978 *234* January 20, pp 68–69, 71, 73–81, 83, 85–90
A series of articles is presented to provide a rounded picture of the package deal approach to construction.
'Hallmark of real change' by R. Warren Evans argues that the system offers a hope for improved performances and indicates the limitations of conventional methods.
'Form of contract' by M. Barnes looks at those significant points for consideration in the development of a standard form of contract, particularly in relation to design responsibility.
A 'Growth Pointers' analyses the extent of the package deal and its potential.

'Company profile' by S. Ashley examines the experiences and attitudes of IDC Ltd.
'Customer appeal' by D. Pearce discusses the advantage and limitations of the client.
'Value for money' by R. Budd illustrates the economic advantages of the package deal and demonstrates the uninspired and mundane design that often results.
'Quality of design' by R. Moxley considers that the design suffers for the sake of economy and that architect directed design/build is often the best solution.
'Pitched just right' by M. Spring suggests that it is possible to introduce innovative design.

176
W. J. Ryder and J. H. Mercer
PROJECT MANAGEMENT
Proc. of ICE Conference 'Management of large capital projects' London 1978, pp 69–82; Discussion pp 83–95
Aspects of project management discussed include contractor selection, contractual conditions, running the job, controlling the design phase, controlling expenditure, the role of the project manager in cost control, controlling the programme and variations.

175
D. S. Barrie and B. C. Paulson, Jr.
'PROFESSIONAL CONSTRUCTION MANAGEMENT'
1978, McGraw-Hill, pp 453
The book is based on US practice and is in three main parts – construction industry and practice; professional construction management in practice; and methods of professional construction management. Within these sections there are chapters dealing with the nature of the industry; development and organisation of a project; preconstruction site investigation, planning scheduling, estimating and design; bidding and aware; selecting a construction manager; project planning and control estimating; cost engineering; procurement; value engineering; quality assurance; and safety and welfare.

174
RICS
'PLACING ORDERS FOR MAJOR CONSTRUCTION WORKS'
1978, pp 6
Methods available to clients for contracting building works are outlined. Reference is made to contractor selection, tendering procedures, types of contract and conditions of contract.

173
RICS
'DESIGN AND BUILD. PACKAGE CONTRACTS WHO REPRESENTS THE CLIENT?'
1978, pp 4
A guidance leaflet giving information on the operation of a package deal and what role the QS may serve.

172
Higgs and Hill
'INTRODUCING THE HIGGS AND HILL MANAGEMENT FEE SERVICE'
1978, pp 12
The project management approach adopted by the company is outlined and examples given of building work carried out under the service.

1977

veyor is then discussed in relation to the cost management and budgeting control services he can provide to project management.

171

DESIGN/CONSTRUCT. TECHNICAL PIONEERING BY DESIGN/CONSTRUCT FIRMS
Civil Engineering 1977 *47* December, pp 76–79
Brief details are given of the projects, particularly in the industrial field, carried out by design/construct firms. Advantages claimed for the technique are summarised.

170
G. Brooke
PROJECT MANAGEMENT IN THE HEALTH SERVICE THE PROBLEMS AND POSSIBLE SOLUTIONS
Hospital Engineering 1977 *31* December, pp 16–20
Having established a definition of project management and the level at which it is practiced in the health service a number of problem interfaces are examined. These include those existing between departments and that between the project team and outside consultants and contractors. Finally some suggestions are made in relation to developing the concept of project management.

169
PROJECT MANAGEMENT IN THE HEALTH SERVICE INVITED CONTRIBUTIONS
Hospital Engineering 1977 *31* December, pp 21–25
Personal views by five individuals are presented on the concept of project management.

168
PROJECT MANAGEMENT IN THE HEALTH SERVICE OPEN FORUM
Hospital Engineering 1977 *31* December, pp 25–26
A summary is presented of the main points raised during discussion.

167
J. Rawlinson and M. Hodgetts
PROJECT MANAGEMENT
Building Economist 1977 *16* December, pp 131–135
The concept and operation of project management are discussed in relation to selection of objectives, establishment of systems, appointment of personnel and organisations, development of work functions and targets and implementation, monitoring and control

166
P. Knowland
ROLE OF THE PROJECT MANAGER
Hospital Development 1977 5 November/December, pp 16–17
The case for the appointment of a project manager to exercise direct control on behalf of the client on project costs and economy. An outline is given of the project managers tasks and duties.

165
D. C. Fulcher
PROJECT MANAGEMENT AND THE QUANTITY SURVEYOR IN AUSTRALIA
Quantity Surveyor 1977 *34* November/December, pp 56–58
Following definitions of the terms 'project manager' and 'construction manager' the recent development of project management is outlined. The role of the quantity sur-

164
W. D. Padget
WHY CONSIDER THE NEED FOR BETTER MANAGEMENT OF HEALTH BUILDING PROJECTS?
Hospital Engineering 1977 *31* November, pp 4–6
It is assumed that the NHS has to ensure that there is no waste of its limited resources and that there is evidence that this has not been achieved in a number of large projects. The concept of project management should be examined further to establish whether it will improve the management of such projects in the future.

163
F. C. Graves
MANAGEMENT THE NATIONAL EXHIBITION CENTRE COMPARED WITH THE HEALTH BUILDING PROJECTS
Hospital Engineering 1977 *31* November, pp 6–8, 11–12
The work of the author as project manager for the NEC is described, the terms of reference for the job and pre- and post-contract activities being highlighted. Some comparisons are made between how it is considered project management should work and how it is not working in the health service.

162
J. Franks
PROJECT MANAGEMENT 9. WORK INVOLVED FROM THE TENDER TO COMPLETION
Building Trades Journal 1977 *174* November 18, pp 30, 32, 34, 36.
The tasks of the project manager are discussed in relation to obtaining tenders, managing the works in progress, controlling costs, handing over and analysing the project.

161
F. C. Graves
CLIENT'S CONTRIBUTION TO A SUCCESSFUL PROJECT MANAGEMENT OPERATION
Proc. Conference Associates Seminar 'Helping the client to build' South AFrica, November 1977, pp 55, 57

160
E. C. Wundram
AMERICAN APPROACH TO CONTRACTING
Paper to CICC Conference 'Management in the Construction Industry' London, November 1977, pp 81–92
A review is made of the common methods of contracting in the USA each method being analysed in terms of definition, selection method, advantages and cautions. The trend to project management is discussed and explained in some detail. Finally, the major differences between British and US contracting are summarised.

159
M. P. Nicholson
CAN A SMALL FIRM INNOVATE?
House Builder 1977 *36* November, pp 451–453
It is suggested that with the development of contracts of the package deal type the builder has a greater interest in innovation since he is intimately associated with the design. The advantage of architects being allowed to become directors of building firms in this respect are

indicated. The concept of innovation is discussed further in relation to prefabricated components, the basis for delays on site, consumer reaction, regulations compliance and time and financial limitations.

158
E. W. McCanlis
CONTRACTUAL OPTIONS IN THE UK
Paper to CICC Conference 'Management in the Construction Industry' London, November 1977, pp 99–111
The financial responsibilities of a contractual situation and the characteristics of contracts are seen to be reflections of project circumstances. The process of arranging a contract is shown to be compounded of separate processes of defining contractual responsibilities, obtaining an offer and selecting a contractor. Each of them are examined in turn. Contracts are classified into types but seen to be composite. The nature of an offer is explored and different types noted and the selection of a contractor is analysed from four viewpoints. Finally, the importance of choosing contractual options, as a function of project management, is related to other aspects of management.

157
S. Kaplan
PROJECT MANAGEMENT: THEORY VERSUS MANAGEMENT
Proc. Conference Associates Seminar 'Helping the client to build' South Africa, November 1977, pp 29, 31, 33, 35, 37–45
The philosophy of project management is expressed before consideration is given to a number of models illustrating number of concepts relative to project management.

156
E. Finsen
ARCHITECT AND PROJECT MANAGEMENT
Proc. Conference Associates Seminar 'Helping the client to build' South Africa, November 1977, pp 21, 23, 25, 27
The relationship between architect and project manager is discussed, the point being made that project management can benefit projects of relatively moderate size. However, this may not be warranted, particularly if the architect is management oriented.

155
F. C. Graves
NATIONAL EXHIBITION CENTRE, BIRMINGHAM, AS AN EXAMPLE OF PROJECT MANAGEMENT
Proc. Conference Associates Seminar 'Helping the client to build' South Africa, November 1977, pp 12–15, 17, 19, 21
An outline is given of the project, reference being made to the terms of reference and pre- and post-contract activities.

154
F. C. Graves
SCOPE AND POTENTIAL OF PROJECT MANAGEMENT IN THE BUILDING INDUSTRY
Proc. Conference Associates Seminar 'Helping the client to build' South Africa, November 1977, pp 3, 5, 7, 9
Consideration is given to defining project management, sources of project managers, functions of project managers, relationships with client and professional team, service agreements; fees and professional indemnity, and recruitment, training and education.

153
J. Franks
PROJECT MANAGEMENT 8. ESTABLISHING GUIDELINES AND PRINCIPLES FOR PROJECTS
Building Trades Journal 1977 *174* October 28, pp 42–44
The tasks of the project manager are enumerated and described in check list form.

152
J. Franks
PROJECT MANAGEMENT 7. DESIGNING, CONSTRUCTING AND DELIVERY TO THE CLIENT
Building Trades Journal 1977 *174* September 30, pp 10, 12The approach to designing the project is considered and the tasks of the contract manager specified in broad terms. The organisation is outlined of a typical management contracting organisation and consideration is given to the problems associated with the closing down of a project.

151
K. Szöke
BUILDING ECONOMICS
Proc. 7th Triennial Congress 'Construction Research International', Edinburgh, September 1977, pp 167–177
In the introduction the position is reviewed of the construction industry in the national economy with special regard to the close interdependence between the general economic situation and the functioning of the construction sector. The impact of recent changes in the economic conditions and policies on the development of the construction industry is discussed briefly regarding both market and planned economies. The conclusion is drawn that while in advanced market economies – due to the recession on the construction market – the process of industrialisation in the construction field has been slowing down, planned economies are invariably heading towards increasing the share of industrialised construction in the total output of the industry. In the second part a few examples are given to illustrate the influence of national/local conditions on the economics of the construction industry. Some general problems affecting the economics of construction are discussed and it is stated that the 'conflicting interests' of the client, the contractor and the designer should be harmonised and, as a reasonable way of facilitating the harmonisation, the application of value analysis methods is recommended. A brief review is given on value analysis/engineering (VA) and on the prerequisites of its application in the construction process. The feasibility of implementing VA is discussed in relation to the traditional and rationalised contracting systems. It is stated that package deal and negotiated contracts provide more favourable conditions for the implementation of VA. Attention is called to certain methodological and information communicational problems concerning the implementation of VA in the construction field.

150
D. S. Barrie and G. L. Muler
PROFESSIONAL CM TEAM DISCOVERS VALUE ENGINEERING
ASCE Journal of the Construction Division 1977 *103* (CO3) September, pp 423–435
The state–of–the–art of traditional value analysis and value engineering methods are reviewed and summarised as developed and utilised by a number of practitioners and agencies on public works. While significant savings have been achieved in the public sector, the value engineering concept has achieved less widespread acceptance in the private domain. The three-party professional construction management concept has facilitated the development of a simplified programme based upon the elimination of adversary relationships often present in the private sector along with the utilisation of the original designer to analyse the technical acceptability of proposed value engineering savings. The simplified approach has produced significant savings on a number of projects and offers promise for increased utilisation on design construct and turnkey projects as well.

149
J. Franks
PROJECTS MANAGEMENT 6. APPLYING THE PRINCIPLES ON CONSTRUCTION PROJECTS
Building Trades Journal 1977 *174* August 12, pp 38–42
Referring to practical examples that tasks of the project manager are seen as mainly being directed towards coordinating, directing, organising and controlling-planning the project, recruiting the team, estimating the project cost, designing the project, construction, handing over, and dissolving the team. The first three of these functions are discussed.

148
PROJECT MANAGEMENT: THE CASE FOR A CODE OF PRACTICE
ICE Proceedings 1977 *62* (Part 1) August, pp 489–502(Discussion)
A number of individual views are expressed on the concept of project management and on the proposal for a code of practice.

147
H. Wattin
METAMORPHOSIS OF A PROJECT MANAGER
Project Manager 1977 *1* July, pp 14–15
The project manager is discussed in the terms of evolution, reference being made to the type of project managed; staff responsibilities; functions; acquiring skills and personal qualities.

146
J. Franks
PROJECT MANAGEMENT 5. HOW THE SYSTEM WORKS WITH THE PROJECT MANAGER
Building Trades Journal 1977 *174* July 8, pp 20, 22, 24, 26, 28
The role and functions of the project manager for the NEC is described to illustrate the principles of the system in practice. This is followed by an analysis of the organisation of a building design partnership, and finally the role of project management in the organisation of turnkey nuclear power projects is discussed.

145
S. H. Wearne
TEACHING PROJECT MANAGEMENT
Project Manager 1977 *1* July, pp 16–17
Brief comments are offered on educational needs, scope of courses, courses offered and the future.

144
A. Bond
SUGGESTED COMPUTER SYSTEM FOR PACKAGE DEAL BUILDING CONTRACTS
Quantity Surveyor 1977 *33* June, pp 199–203
It is argued that the full potential of the computer cannot be realised with the present system of contracting but that it can be achieved where the greater part of the design and construction work is carried out by one organisation. The applications of a computer within the package deal concept are then described.

143
A. C. Maevis
PROS AND CONS OF CONSTRUCTION MANAGEMENT
ASCE Journal of the Construction Division 1977 *103* (CO1) June, pp 169–177
With an increase in the size and complexity of construction projects a need has arisen for a more professional approach to the overall management of these projects. Construction management has grown out of this need. A series of case histories is presented, both successful and unsuccessful. In the analysis and conclusion a series of ground rules are presented describing the owner's and the construction manager's responsibility in the process.

142
J. Franks
PROJECT MANAGEMENT 4. USA CONSTRUCTS BUILDINGS QUICKER THAN BRITAIN
Building Trades Journal 1977 *173* May 27, pp 16, 18, 20, 22
The concept of project management as practiced in the US is described. This is followed by a brief comparison between the contracting organisation in the UK and US and an analysis of the reason for failure. Finally, the organisation of contracting as effected by the Public Building Service is discussed. In this system the client is played by the project manager and the architect is occupied with the design and with the packaging of working drawings and specifications to fit the most advantageous grouping of separate construction contracts selected.

141
J. Sims
WHERE OUR SYSTEM GOES WRONG
Building 1977 *232* May 6, p 73
It is argued that the present system of contracting mitigates against efficiency. Although the system is better, more flexible and sophisticated than that used in the USA therein lies its disadvantages since this removes the essential element of discipline. One of the main factors limiting efficiency is regarded as the letting of contracts on incomplete design information.

140
J. Franks
PROJECT MANAGEMENT 3. GREATER INVOLVEMENT IN EUROPEAN CONSTRUCTION WORK
Building Trades Journal 1977 *173* April 22, pp 22, 24, 26, 28
A survey is made of the construction processes in France, West Germany and Sweden to illustrate the principal differences between the organisation structures used. This survey is made with particular reference to design, construction organisation and control; cost control; and construction and contract procedures. Finally the situation in these countries is compared with the European countries to ascertain the state of the art of project management in Europe generally.

139
PROJECT MANAGEMENT
Chartered Surveyor 1977 *109* April, pp 290–292
General principles are set out that are likely to apply in project management, particular attention being given to the definition of project management, sources of the project manager, project management services, relationships, service agreements, fees and professional indemnity, and recruitment and training. Finally, a check list is presented which represents the main points which a project manager should ensure are dealt with either personally or by other members of the professional team.

138
CHANGING BUILDING INDUSTRY
Construction 1977 *49* April, pp 21, 40–41
This overview of the trends in the US building industry considers the impact of insurance – liability and completed operations cover in particular – the building systems approach adopted by the General Services Administration for public buildings, and management contracting

137
R. W. Evans
PROPERTY AND PROPER ECONOMY. CAN THEY BE RECONCILED IN LOCAL AUTHORITY HOUSE PRODUCTION?
Chartered Surveyor Building and Quantity Surveyor Quarterly 1977 *4* Spring, pp 38–39
The argument is advanced that conventional tendering procedures on the basis of full drawings, bills of quantities and competitive selection have three major defects. These are that 20% of the expenditure is outside control they are weak in controlling actual expenditure; and they contain no management check on contract extensions and variations. Non-conventional methods, it is argued, should not be ignored since they can be controlled by use of the generic performance specification.

136
J. Franks
PROJECT MANAGEMENT 2. THE REVIVAL OF THE PROJECT MANAGER IN CONSTRUCTION
Building Trades Journal 1977 *173* March 25, pp 20, 22, 24
The development of management contracting and of the project manager in particular in the 1960's is discussed with reference to the appropriate literature.

135
F. Hotson
HOUSING. DESIGN AND BUILD. A MONEY SAVER FOR LOCAL AUTHORITIES
Building Trades Journal 1977 *173* March 25, pp 10–12, 14
The design and build approach adopted by Shanley Contracting is described and its application to local authority contracts is discussed. It is claimed that the tendering system allows rapid start and completion of a project within the housing cost yardstick and yet to Parker Morris Standards.

134
J. Franks
PROJECT MANAGEMENT 1. NEW ROLE OF CO-ORDINATOR IS STILL EVOLVING
Building Trades Journal 1977 *173* February 25, pp 11–12, 14, 16
Views from a number of sources are gathered to explore what is meant by project management, and these are considered in relation to the conventional relationships between the members of the building team.

133
P. Makepeace
PLATFORM: PACKAGE DEALS
Building Design 1977 February 18, p 18
The cost and time effectiveness of package deals is challenged, arguments being presented in favour of the architect controlled project.

132
A. C. Sidwell
PROJECT MANAGEMENT AND MEASUREMENT IN SWEDEN
Building Technology and Mangement 1977 *15* February, pp 14–15, 25
Following a short outline of the Swedish building industry, consideration is given to the responsibility for building failure and the provision of quantity surveying services. The management contracting system (byggledare) is described, its main advantages being highlighted.

131
M. Snowdon
PROJECT MANAGEMENT: THE CASE FOR A CODE OF PRACTICE
ICE Proc. 1977 *62* (Part 1) February, pp 43–50
The wide issues embraced by the term project management are acknowledged but limits are suggested for the purpose of discussion. It is suggested that formalisation of some of the activity within the concept could improve the professionalism of the work, strengthen the links between the academic and the practical, provide a firmer base for training and experience and improve the understanding which is necessary to establish optimum organisations. A preliminary scope for a code of practice is suggested as a basis for presenting the case.

130
D. O. Pedersen
DESIGN CONSTRUCTION PROJECTS: GETTING VALUE FOR MONEY
Build International 1977 *5* January/February, pp 24–33 (in English and French)
The application of value analysis techniques are described

1976

in relation to project management contracts. Value analysis can be employed to choose from several proposals on the basis of a comprehensive assessment of quality and cost (and time); to guide the design toward defined goals; and to improve communication between client and designer.

129
D. O. Pedersen
DESIGN CONTRACT PROJECTS: GETTING VALUE FOR MONEY
Building Research and Practice 1977 5 January/February, pp 24–33 (in English and French)
Value analysis techniques are described as they are applied in Scandinavia to promote new building methods, improve design and contracting procedures and provide better value for money to the client.

128
G. Trickey
DEVELOP AND CONSTRUCT
Architects Journal 1977 165 January 26, pp s177–178
Develop and construct contracts are those in which the architect prepares sketch designs from the brief, determines site layout, disposition of building on site and the individual plan forms. The contractor develops this proposal, making final choices of materials and details, before submitting his tender. Advantages of the system are evaluated and some reservations expressed. It is concluded that efficiency can be best improved by builders concentrating on site management and by architects becoming more sensitive to the requirements of efficient construction when developing their designs.

127
M. Snowdon
'MANAGEMENT OF ENGINEERING PROJECTS'
1977, Newnes-Butterworth, pp 134
Attention is given to project management, regarded as 'the achievement of an objective by the creation of a new or the modification of an existing capital asset', and considered to cover the total project from concept through to commissioning. Chapters are included on setting the scene; the anatomy of a project; management needs; planning the action; monitoring and controlling the action; people; and looking forward. Appendices deal with the time value of money; risk analysis; and project date for a chemical plant and swimming bath.

126
S. Goldhaber, C. K. Jha and M. C. Macedo Jr.
'CONSTRUCTION MANAGEMENT PRINCIPLES AND PRACTICES'
1977, John Wiley and Sons, pp 312
The concept of construction (project) management (CM) is introduced and defined and this is followed by a description of those principles and practices that make the concept work. Chapters are included on methodologies; advanced computer-based scheduling and cost control techniques; value management; field organisation; contractual aspects; case studies; and outlook for CM.

125
D. Barclay
FUTURE ROLE OF THE QS
Building 1976 231 November 12, p 110
The view is expressed that not only is the QS profession unsuited to an expansionist role (into management contracting) but an investigation of their present activities and eventual curtailment to meet modern methods would improve generally the overall performances of the industry. Two areas of concern which are discussed relate to services, particularly bill preparation, and to fees.

124
R. P. Harris
TIME ELEMENT (PART 2)
Quantity Surveyor 1976 33 November, pp 69–75
Consideration is given to the relative performance of architect designed and package deal contracts in terms of construction time, post-completion time and overall time. The financial implications of time are discussed with reference to cost as a function of time, project details and times, construction prices, and optimum time. It is concluded that if the client is seeking to occupy his factory within the shortest possible time then the package deal will generally be the most appropriate.

123
R. P. Harris
THE TIME ELEMENT (PART 1)
Quantity Surveyor 1976 33 October, pp 49–55
An analysis is made of competitive tendered and package deal alternatives for traditionally constructed factory buildings with the aim of establishing the time performance of each system and the ramification of such findings. Initially, consideration is given to client priorities and constraints from which it is concluded that clients give a high priority to the time element. This is followed by a report of the investigation of the time period of the pre-construction period of the contracts. From this it is concluded that a package dealer would provide a higher probability of achieving programmed design dates.

122
M. V. Manzoni
CONSTRUCTION OF THE NATIONAL EXHIBITION CENTRE
Polytechnic Seminar 'Professional Project Control', Birmingham, October 6, 1976 pp 74–78
The role of the project controller during the construction phase is briefly discussed under the headings construction difficulties, specific and contractual problems, definitions, and functions.

121
E. D. Mills
DESIGN OF THE NATIONAL EXHIBITION CENTRE
Proc. City of Birmingham Polytechnic Seminar 'Professional Project Control', Birmingham, October 6, 1976 pp 68–71; Discussion pp 72–73
Some general comments are made on the initiation and construction aspects of Centre, the problem areas being highlighted.

120

B. G. Lund

INTRODUCTION TO THE NATIONAL EXHIBITION CENTRE

Proc. City of Birmingham Polytechnic Seminar 'Professional Project Control', Birmingham, October 6, 1976 pp 61–67

The historical background to the NEC and its evolution in its present form are outlined. The process of preparing the brief is described and this is followed by an analysis of the reasons for employing a project manager. The lessons gained at NEC are discussed with particular reference to co-ordination of a large design team and the need for complete control and discipline against a background of full co-operation from all concerned and a rigid financial control.

119

A. F. Adair

PROJECT MANAGEMENT AND PROJECT CONTROL

Proc. City of Birmingham Polytechnic Seminar 'Professional Project Control', Birmingham, October 6, 1976, pp 17–38; Discussion pp 39–41

The role of project management is seen as being responsible for a project from inception to completion and as such being responsible for the preparation of a plan which will enable the objectives of the project to be achieved. The second phase of the project manager's role is controlling the project when the plan is implemented. Team management structures are considered prior to a closer examination of the role and need for a project manager. Finally, skills and abilities of the project manager are analysed.

118

A. G. J. Desssewffy

IN SEARCH OF THE 'IDEAL' CONSTRUCTION CONTRACT

Building Economist 1976 *15* September, pp 69–78

Recent developments are outlined in the documentation and administration of building and civil engineering contracts, particular reference being made to British practice under the headings – lump sum contracts (including two-stage tendering, negotiated and serial tendering, management contracting, package deals, formula price adjustment) and cost reimbursable contracts (fixed fee and prime cost contracts and target and cost reimbursable contracts). The relevance of these procedures to the Australian building industry is discussed.

117

D. S. Barrie and B. C. Paulson Jr.

PROFESSIONAL CONSTRUCTION MANAGEMENT

ASCE Journal of the Construction Division 1976 *102* (CO3) September, pp 425–436

The findings and conclusions of ASCE's Task Committee on Management of Construction Projects are reported. Definitions of 'Professional Construction Management' and 'Professional Construction Manager' and the reasoning behind them are explained. The responsibilities are then described of the professional construction manager and his requirements in the planning and execution phases of a project. Professional construction management

differs from conventional design-construct and traditional separate contractor and designer approaches in that there are by definition three separate and distinct members of the team (owner, designer, and manager) and the professional construction manager does not perform significant design or construction work with his own forces. Professional construction management is not necessarily better or worse than other methods of procuring constructed facilities. However, the three-party-team approach is certainly a viable alternative to more traditional methods in many applications as its increasing use demonstrates.

116

J. Johns

PROJECT MANAGEMENT

Building Economist 1976 *15* September, pp 87–93

This paper is presented in the form of a conversation between three project managers and discusses the role of the project manager and the reasons for his appointment by the client, and some typical problems.

115

L. G. Krantz

MANAGEMENT IN HIGH RISK AREAS

Quantity Surveyor 1976 *33* September, pp 26–29

The need for owner-oriented project management is considered prior to a discussion of the requirements for better management tools, particular attention being given to deficiencies in conventional schedule and cost analysis.

114

WHO'S IN CHARGE HERE?

Building 1976 *230* June 25, pp 92–93

The basic advantages of management contracting are examined to draw attention to some of its limitations. In conclusion it is stated that the contractor is suited to a more prominent part than the principles of project management consultancy permit.

113

A. V Kocass and G. French

CONSTRUCTION MANAGEMENT

Paper to the 25th Conference of the Building Science Forum of Australia (NSW Division) Sydney, June 9 1976, pp 8

Project management as offered by a contracting organisation is described, reference being made to method and terms of engagement, contractual arrangements, documentation, client's brief and budget, time, cost and finance control, team selection and construction and commissioning of the project.

112

K. A. Hawson, R. G. Brookes and G. A. Sutherland

PROJECT MANAGER (CLIENT)

Paper to 25th Conference of the Building Science Forum of Australia (NSW Division) Sydney, June 9 1976, pp 12

The presentation is in the form of discussions between the three authors. They consider the role of project manager/client (i.e. project managers appointed to client's staff) and why clients make this appointment. Some of the problem areas are identified.

111
I. Turner
PROJECT MANAGEMENT SERVICES
Paper to the 25th Conference of the Building Science Forum of Australia (NSW Division) Sydney, June 9 1976, pp 11
The role of the project management consultant is outlined, his evolution, the advantages and disadvantages, and the methods employed being considered. Attention is then given to contractual arrangements, the client brief, documentation and construction.

110
T. Crow and R. Hammond
MANAGEMENT CONSULTANT PROJECT MANAGEMENT
Paper to 25th Conference of the Building Science Forum of Australia (NSW Division) Sydney, June 9 1976, pp 12
The case is argued for the management consultant to improve the co-ordination of and communication between members of the building team. The detailed role of such consultants is described, reference being made to benefits, basis of engagement, client's brief, sketch plan, design development, working drawings, construction and commissioning.

109
W. J. Diepeveen
PROJECT MANAGEMENT THROUGH BUILDING TEAMS
Proc. CIB Symposium on Organisation and Management of Construction Washington, May 1976a, pp 36–49
The value is discussed of the use of matrix organisation to co-ordinate the functions of the building team members. It makes use of the optimal motivation of each member by treating him as an equal and independent expert, responsible for his own work, but acting with others in a team in the interest of an optimal project constructed during the course of an optimal process. A matrix organisation is a mixed structure. Carrying on from this concept of project management (management contracting) is considered, the structure being identified and management of the management of the process outlined.

108
D. J. O. Ferry
DEVELOPING TRENDS IN THE PROCUREMENT OF BUILDINGS
Building Economist 1976 *14* March, pp 216–220
The organisational problems are considered of the client in acquiring a building and those factors are identified which have led to conventional contractual arrangements being regarded as less than satisfactory. Alternative methods discussed are negotiated contracts, the package deal and management contracting. Each method is evaluated, its advantages and limitations being indicated.

107
Associated General Contractors of America
'CONSTRUCTION MANAGEMENT CONTROL PROCESS'
1976, pp 6 (**9** flow charts)
Guidelines are presented to indicate the normal processes to be followed on a CM project. The process is represented by the following three flow charts:
Division of responsibility for performance
Responsibility flow
Project control by the construction manager.

106
A. Walker
'PROJECT MANAGEMENT A REVIEW OF THE STATE OF THE ART'
1976, IQS, pp 76
A review is made of recent developments in the structure of the arrangements for the management of construction projects on behalf of the client. It considers the role and responses of project management from inception through the life of the building. The current state of development of project management as a separately identifiable function is considered through interviews with 18 organisations and conclusions are drawn in respect of the art and the possible directions project management may take. Developments in project management are considered against the performance of conventional processes.

105
US General Services Administration
'USING CONSTRUCTION MANAGEMENT FOR PUBLIC AND INSTITIONAL FACILITIES'
1976, pp 73
A study of the use of project management (PM) by state and local agencies has shown that it has achieved general acceptance and that most users (73%) would consider using it again. The usefulness of PM increases in proportion to project complexity and cost; the total PM approach can be used on a cost effective basis for complex projects with costs of $3 million and above. On the other hand individual features, such as value analysis, may yield real cost benefits on projects costing $1 million or less. The several forms of PM are described and a guide is provided to public administrations to allow them to determine whether or how they want to use PM.

104
N. H. Heayes
TAKING THE WRAPS OFF THE BUILDING 'PACKAGE'
Contract Journal 1976 *270* April 29, pp 24–25
A general look is taken at recent developments in non-traditional contractual procedures, such as develop and construct, and the package deal. EArly involvement of the contractor in the contract is discussed.

103
G. T. Heery and E. M. Davies
CONSTRUCTION PROGRAMME MANAGEMENT
Building Technology and Management 1976 *14* April, pp 22–26
Construction programme management is defined as 'that group of management activities over and above normal architectural and engineering services related to a construction programme, carried out during the pre-design, and construction phases, that provides control of time and cost in the construction of a new facility'. The professional manager is thereby one who associates with the client to apply the proper combination of management techniques to achieve time and cost control. The role of this project

manager is classified into ten basic components which are each considered in turn; pre-decision programming and budgetting; selection of designers and preparation of design contracts; pre-design project analysis; early cost and methods analysis; integrated cost control procedures; design review and approvals; time control procedures; computer assisted scheduling; management of tender/award; management during construction.

102
L. J. Brown
APLICATION OF MANAGEMENT METHODS IN DESIGN/CONSTRUCTION
Proc. CIB Symposium on Organisation and Management of Construction Washington, May 1976, pp IV–85–IV–95
An outline is given of the contractual procedures employed by the Canadian Department of Defence. They are fixed price contracts:
(i) traditional (design – bid – build)
(ii) Proposal call (performance specification. bid – design – build).
and construction management contracts:
(i) project management/construction management
(ii) design – bid 7– build sequentially(iii) design – bid – build with pre-tendering

101
D. C. Aird and V. K. Handa
CREATING FLEXIBILITY IN A CONVENTIONAL DESIGN/CONSTRUCT ORGANISATION
Proc. CIB Symposium on Organisation and Management of Construction
Washington, May 1976, pp 1–15
The development processes involved with a design/construct organisation responsible for the construction of fossil fuelled and nuclear power stations are described. A matrix organisation – part functional, part profit type – was selected; the advantages and limitations of this organisation are outlined.

1975

100
H. Buteux
DESIGN AND BUILD THE SSHA's ANSWER
Architects Journal 1975 *162* December 3, pp 1169–1170
The Scottish Special Housing Association's methods described are claimed to speed up housing contracts by using the design team to accelerate pre-contract documentation. It involves transferring the decision on forms of construction from the contractor to the design team and by rationalising the details used in house building – using an open-ended library of standard details.

99
G. S. Birrell
'BUYING' A NEW BUILDING: THE US MANAGEMENT APPROACH
Chartered Surveyor Building and Quantity Surveying quarterly 1975/76 *3* Winter, pp 23–28
the requirement of a client for a new building is used to explore the methods employed to ensure its constitution. Attention is devoted to the selection of the project team, comprising in this case separate design and construction firms. In addition a construction manager representing

the client was appointed. Following on, consideration is given to the selection of bidding sub-contractors, project control during design and construction, sub-contractor control on site, and interim payments to sub-contractors. Finally, those major points are discussed, which lead to successful management of 'buying' a building.

98
S. E. Smith et al
CONTRACTUAL RELATIONSHIPS IN CONSTRUCTION
ASCE Proc. Journal of the Construction Division 1975 *101* (CO4) December, pp 907–921
The different types of contractual relationship in the US are considered from the owner, consultant, contractor and legal viewpoints. Principal relationships considered are general contractor, turnkey, construction manager and independent prime contracts.

97
A. H. Barraclough
FEE TYPE CONTRACTS
Building 1975 *229* November 28, pp 78
Experience, up to the conclusion of the pre-contract stage, is reported of the Department of Architecture and Planning of Leeds City Council providing most of the architectural services for a fee type contract.
Particular aspects discussed include contract options, estimate of prime cost, interviewing contractors, and the spread of tenders received.

96
SHOULD RIBA TIE IN WITH THE PACKAGE DEAL?
Contract Journal 1975 *268* November 27, p 22
It is considered that the cost of construction is too high and that the refinements, that the separation of design and construction entails, can no longer be afforded. It is suggested that the RIBA should revise its rules of conduct by allowing its members to become company directors.

95
M. J. D Keatings
SOLVING THE COMMUNICATION PROBLEM
Building 1975 *229* August 29, pp 43–45
It is considered that the trend in the development of the JCT standard form of contract has been a progressive transfer of risk from the contractor to the employer, exemplified by the relative lack of involvement of the architect during construction. Areas of difficulty identified are associated with design to co-ordination and nominated sub-contracts. It is advocated that on large or complex projects the client should appoint his own project manager. Consideration should also be given to the suitability of the JCT form of contract.

94
K. Manson
LIABILITY IN A PACKAGE DEAL CONTRACT
Building Trades Journal 1975 *170* July 25, pp 14, 16, 18
The case is reported of *Greaves & Co (Contractors) v Baynham, Meikle & Partners* from which the following conclusions are drawn:
(a) Where there is a package deal contact the contractor is liable to the client if the building is not reasonably fit for its intended use.
(b) Architects/engineers are obliged to use reasonable

care and skill in their professional duties.

(c) In such circumstances a professional man in his duties implies a warranty that the design will be fit for the intended purpose.

(d) A contractor employing a professional whose designs are not fit for the purpose may be able to obtain indemity for the cost of works to prevent and rectify damage.

93

SURPRISE PACKAGE

Architect 1975 *12* July, pp 16–18

The P.O. Telecommunications Centre at Carlisle was constructed under a package deal contract by IDC Limited, and completed in 32 months – half the usual time.

92

H. Cruickshank

QUANTITY SURVEYOR/CONTRACTOR BARRIER: SOME HOME TRUTHS

Chartered Surveyor Building and Quantity Surveying Quarterly 1975 *2* Summer, pp 45, 47–49

It is considered that the standard competitive system of placing contracts is the central cause of existing barriers, and evidence is presented to support this view. To resolve the situation it is suggested that the consultant must persuade the client of the value of more accountable integrated design construction teams and contract procedures.

91

REPORT OF NON-TRADITIONAL METHODS OF CONTRACTING

Building Economist 1975 *14* June, pp 1, 3–13

This report was prepared by Australian IQS Contractual Relations Committee. It covers the conventional forms of contract – lump sum and cost reimbursement – and attempts to assess the relative merits and disadvantages in relation to non-traditional methods; particular attention being given to the problems of the design team, public accountability and pre-contract consultative services. Appendices provide suggested principles for selecting a contractor; details of the factors considered in determination of price; and details of non-traditional contractual methods – provisional lump sum and negotiated contract types.

90

CONSULTANTS ENGINEERS LIABLE TO CONTRACTORS IN PACKAGE DEAL

Times 1975 May 16. p8

On appeal it was held that in the case of *Greaves & Co. (Contractors) Ltd. v Baynham. Meikle and Partners* that contractors are entitled to a declaration of liability and an indemnity from consultants for the cost of work necessary to prevent and rectify damage to a building built under a package deal contract.

89

W. Amos and P M. Worthington

MULTI–DISCIPLINARY PROJECT MANAGEMENT

ICE Proceedings 1975 *58* (Part 1) May, pp 305–310

The various aspects are summarised that establish the viability of project management. One view is expressed that specialists and project management should receive the same opportunities and rewards, thereby promoting the concept of matrix management – the practice where

a consultant reports to a superior in his own firm on technical and administrative matters and to the client on matters concerning the project. A need for formal training in project management is identified.

88

D. D. Patterson

PROJECT MANAGEMENT AND THE ENGINEER

ICE Proceedings 1975 *58* (Part 1) May, pp 205–211

With complex projects clients are requiring more detailed information on programme/performance and expenditure/budget and in consequence the engineer has to develop monitoring techniques to supply these data. The interaction of the activities of project managers, client, contractors and engineers is reviewed with particular reference to the obligations imposed by the General Conditions of Contract.

87

M. Barnes

PROJECT MANAGER – A MAN OR A MYTH?

New Civil Engineer 1975 May 29. pp 22

It is considered that if the American view of project management as a new and definable concept is correct then it must differ from the British attitude since it does not appear to embrace any new techniques, relying as it does on the application of conventional techniques for cost control and planning and scheduling. Consequently it is suggested that its strength must lie in attitudes – the completion on time and within a budget being pre-eminent aims which are not merged with those of producing an elegant or functional design. Indications are given that there will be an increased demand in the UK for project management as clients stress the importance of conserving time and money.

86

M. Laing

PACKAGE DEAL – THE COMPLETE ANSWER?

Paper to IOB/PSA Conference 'Getting buildings designed and built – can we afford today's ways?' London, April 1975, pp 11

The importance is stressed of providing buildings that represent the best possible value for money. The package deal, applied to suitable projects, is considered to meet this aim provided that the client who does not regularly buy new buildings, retains independent professional advice. Package deals can increase the efficiency with which a project is completed and substantial savings can be obtained from bringing design into the area of competition and by giving proper consideration to the most effective method of construction. Package deals are widely used abroad and increasingly so in the UK – the contractor has a responsibility to see that they are used to benefit the client and the community.

85

R. I. Northern

CLIENT MANAGED PROJECTS – A COMPLETE SERVICE

Paper to IOB/PSA Conference 'Getting buildings designed and built – can we afford today's ways?' London, April 1975. pp7

Based on practical experience the aspects of project management discussed include the client's responsibilities, the function of the project manager, the alternative forms of contract, selection, integration of the building team, monitoring techniques, and final appraisal of the completed building.

84
W. Amos
INTRODUCING THE SUBJECT

Paper to IOB/PSA Conference 'Getting buildings designed and built – can we afford today's ways?' London, April 1975, pp 7

The current interest in project management is reviewed. This is followed by an outline of the organisation of project teams and analysis of the four stages involved in the building process which require special skills and involve different proportions of the total cost. The client's role is briefly considered prior to a summary of the methods of dealing with the management of projects. Attention is drawn to various fields of activities by listing the action programme of the PSA as a typical example of the amount of involvement in a client/designer organisation. Finally the services are suggested that clients should receive from the industry throughout the building process.

83
A. F. Sampson
CONSTRUCTION MANAGEMENT – THE GSA APPROACH

Paper to IOB/PSA Conference 'Getting buildings designed and built – can we afford today's ways?' London, April 1975. pp 19

The GSA (General Services Agency) provides for the civilian agencies of the US Government a system for the management of property and records, including construction and the operation and protection of buildings. One division of the GSA is the Public Buildings Service and an account is given of the management techniques employed by the service, as developed over the past five years. The current state of the US building industry is indicated and some thoughts expressed on future trends in the built environment.

82
G. T Heery
CONSTRUCTION MANAGEMENT IN ACTION

Paper to IOB/PSA Conference 'Getting buildings designed and built – can we afford today's ways?' London, April 1975. pp 8

Attention is focussed on the services of the independent construction manager (US practice) and details are given of how the manager utilises the time/cost control system from pre-design through to occupancy. Specific case histories are reviewed which illustrate the scope of projects, the schedules and cost accomplished and the construction management plan in relation to phasing etc.

81
A. T. Brett-Jones
'WHICH BUILDER?'. TENDERING PROCEDURES AND CONTRACTUAL ARRANGEMENTS

Paper to RICS 10th Triennial Conference of Quantity Surveyors, London, April 1975, pp 17

It is advocated that tendering is an essential and key factor in the economic use of building resources and that decisions on tendering are essentially matters of professional advice which is primarily the responsibility of the quantity surveyor. Clients too often regard themselves as expert in tendering, a function which may have as great an effect as design-decisions on the resources used in a building project. In considering the economic use of building resource four main aspects are identified: the contractor's effect on design; production cost savings; continuity; and risk. The significance of public accountability in formulating tendering policy is also indicated. The principles and application of negotiated and competitive tendering and fixed price and cost reimbursement contracts are discussed and some alternative forms, such as the package deal, identified. It is suggested that a tender should be evaluated not only in terms of the price offered but also in terms of the investment to be made and the potential saving if continuation contracts are negotiated. Such savings would need to be quantified by the identification and measurement of productivity. The close involvement of the client and the need to control sub-contractors tends towards the management contracting situation. In this the quantity surveyor would play a significant role.

80
K. Terry
CONTRACTUAL ARRANGEMENTS AND TENDERING PROCEDURES IN THE BUILDING INDUSTRY

Build 1975 *11* April, pp 12, 14–15

An outline is given of the most common forms of contractual arrangements and tendering procedures.

79
W. James
PROJECT MANAGEMENT

Building Economist 1975 *13* March, pp 200–204

Project management is discussed in relation to eight sections defining the function. These sections involve:

(a) Defining and obtaining the client's agreement to physical and financial objectives, priorities, delegation of power to the project manager, requirements as to frequency of reports etc. and terms of appointment.

(b) Selection and appointment of consultants capable of achieving the client's objectives.

(c) Settling terms of appointment of all consultants and the forms of agreement for executing the works.

(d) Checking and co-ordinating budgets and programme, formulation of global budget, monitoring and reporting progress.

(e) Organising and reporting on arrangements for running and maintenance of the finished works.

(f) Reporting at completion of works on the financial outcome of the project.

78
T. Mitchell
IN PRAISE OF PACKAGE DEALS

Building Design 1975 February 21, pp 20–21

The management approach of IDC Consultants to package deals is outlined and some practical examples of the advantages of the system indicated.

77
P. Grafton
QS MARK II THE NEW HORIZONS

Building 1975 *228* February 14, pp 66–67

Some individual thoughts are expressed on the quantity surveyor as project manager and on the general contribution the RICS can make to planning and construction.

76
A. P. Grant
ECONOMICS OF THE PACKAGE DEAL
Building 1975 *228* January 31, pp 68 (Correspondence)
The advantages, in particular for industrial building, of the package deal are outlined.

75
DOE
'DEVELOP AND CONSTRUCT'
1975, HMSO, pp 44
The develop and construct procedure is divided into eight stages with the design and construct phases overlapping. The architect remains responsible for the design but the contractor is given a share of the professional effort required for detailed work and can begins site work while this is continuing. The work is carried out using the contractor's own building method whereas the architect's skill is employed in producing type plans for all the buildings and arranging them on the site. The professional effort of the contractor lies in adapting his method to the type plans and to the site in a manner acceptable to the architect. Significant time savings are made using the procedure. Following a case study, flow charts are presented illustrating the sequence of operations-feasibility, sketch design, working drawings and specifications, bills of quantities, tender period, evaluation and acceptance of tender, develop, construct.

74
O. Lindgrew et al
EARLY TENDERING FOR PLUMBING INSTALLA-TIONS ACCORDING TO THE FEE METHOD
National Swedish Building Research Summary R19: 1975, pp 2
This summary considered the early negotiation of plumbing contracts by the fee method. Indications are provided of the time savings achieved and other aspects of the report such as the assessment of the relative proportions of labour, material and other costs, and product group breakdown for different contracts.

73
Hillier Parker May and Rowden
'PROPERTY DEVELOPMENT – SUMMARY OF PRO-FESSIONAL AND ESTATE SERVICES'
1975, pp 24
A brochure providing some reasons for the use of management contracting and some examples of where it has been successfully employed.

72
G. T. Heery
'TIME, COST AND ARCHITECTURE'
1975, McGraw Hill, pp 212
A definitive system is discussed for time and cost content that may be applied within any programme of requirements, quality level or design goal. The time/cost control system can be employed by the architect/engineer or by the construction manager. Both approaches are considered. Commencing with fourteen case histories further chapters deal with a management approach to the construction programme: the client; introduction to time/ cost control system; pre-design project analysis; systems approach

to design; cost-control system; time control, contract time provision and extension rulings; use of CPM and scheduling techniques; phased, separate and transferable contracts; bid and negotiations management; and construction management in the construction phase.

71
NEDO:
'THE PUBLIC CLIENT AND THE CONSTRUCTION INDUSTRIES'
1975, HMSO. pp 126
It is fond that public clients tend to view each project in isolation rather than in relation to their on-going programmes of work. This does not make for the most efficient use of clients' or contractors' resources. Studies showed that value for money is construed too narrowly and sought largely in the wrong place – it is looked for primarily at the letting of individual projects. The end of 'stop-go' policies is called for and the Government is urged to adopt policies to foster greater stability in demand, and to keep a watchful eye upon the supply of funds. The important role of the client is stressed. Design and construct contracts were found to perform well and the advantages were established of the contractor participating in the pre-construction phases. Open tendering is condemned and two stage tendering is advocated for one-off projects of large scale or complexity, 'design and construct' for repetitive projects; and serial tenders for continuous programmes of similar projects. A look is taken at payment and disputes on construction contracts and although limited remedies only are advanced it is recommended that a mini-tender could be used whereby the contractor, faced with a major variation, quotes an inclusive price for its execution, the client being given the option of accepting the price or of pricing the variation under the conventional procedures. The provision is also suggested of calling in an independent expert to ascertain the facts in a dispute.

1974

70
PSA WAY – DEVELOP AND CONSTRUCT
Building 1974 *227* November 15, pp 141, 143
The develop and construct procedure described involves contractors offering tenders on the basis of site layouts, plan types and performance specifications. The successful tenderer is given possession of the site while the contractor in parallel prepares the working drawings which are vetted by the project architect. One of the main advantages is the overall time savings from sketch design to completion and the early involvement of the selected contractor. The eight conventional stages involved in the contract are outlined.

69
A. Massey
PROJECT MANAGEMENT – A NEW APPROACH
Paper to IOB Annual Conference, London, November 1974, pp 5
The basic parameters of project management are defined and the value of this type of service to the client described. Education and training requirements are indicated and future prospects discussed.

68

G. B. Wheeldon

FACTORY BUILDING – ADVANTAGES OF THE PACKAGE DEAL

Building Trades Journal 1974 *168* October 25, pp 28, 31, 33–35

The principles of operation of a package deal contract are described and the advantage to both client and builder summarised.

67

W. James

PROJECT MANAGEMENT

Chartered Surveyor, Building & Quantity Surveying Quarterly 1974 *2* Autumn, pp 1–4

A definition is given of project management in relation to a construction-development project. This definition is classified into eight sections and these are discussed separately. They involved (a) establishing the clients requirements (b) selecting and appointing consultants able to achieve the clients objectives (c) settling terms of appointment of all consultants and the forms of agreement for executing the works (d) checking and co-ordinating initial individual budgets and programmes, and testing their validity (e) organising and reporting on arrangements for running and maintenance of finished works, including documentation (f) reporting at completion of works on the financial outcome of the project.

66

S. Lucas

TIME SAVING AT A FAIR PRICE

Building 1974 *227* September 13. pp 123, 125

Following an outline of the disadvantage that can be experienced by competitive tendering the benefits of negotiated contracts, package deals and the management fee system are summarised. It is considered that whereas the client is unlikely to get a cheaper building he is likely to be occupying it much quicker.

65

W. T. Shaw

MANAGEMENT CONTRACTORS? OR 'BRASS PLATE' BUILDERS?

Surveying Technician 1974 *3* June, pp 8–10

The differences in contracting between pre and post-war contracting are outlined and some possible reasons for these are indicated. A schedule is presented of the make-up of a contract sum for a contract in the 1930's compared to one of today which illustrates the considerable reduction in the work carried out directly by the contractor.

64

J. R. Lowe

POINTS AGAINST PACKAGE DEAL

Construction News 1974 March 28, pp 8 (Correspondence)

One main criticism is the inability to use the strengths of specialists to the best purpose. This is reinforced by the view that an independent consulting engineer can provide a better service.

63

G. R. Hill

AGAINST THE PACKAGE DEAL

Construction News 1974 March 14, pp 29

Construction News 1974 March 21, pp 10 (missing illustration)

It is claimed that the vast majority of package deal contracts are typified by a low standard of design and value for money. Costs are considered to be 10–20% more expensive than a conventional contract plus professional fees. Particular attention is given to the apparent inadequate specification found with such contracts.

62

P. W. G. Morris

SYSTEMS STUDY OF PROJECT MANAGEMENT – 2

Building 1974 *226* February 1, pp 83–84, 87–88

The systems approach to project management is discussed with particular reference to integration, co-ordination and control, the overall co-ordination of design and production, and production.

61

P. W. G Morris

SYSTEMS STUDY OF PROJECT MANAGEMENT – 1

Building 1974 *226* January 25, pp 75–76. 79–80

Research is reported on the various types of design/production, interface which exist in building using analytical techniques belonging to organisations and systems theory. The case studies presented cover a traditional contract, two negotiated contracts and three where there was closer involvement of design and construction such as management fee, and management contracting.

60

J. C. White

IMPROVED BUILDING PROCUREMENT MEANS A CHANGED BUILDING PROCESS

Industrialisation Forum 1974 *5* (1–2), pp 39–43

Related to US practice the broad process problems experienced by the client, designer, contractor, sub-contractor, and the manufacturer are outlined. Limitations in the traditional bidding process are considered and some alternatives – negotiated contract, phased bidding and construction – are indicated: both require project management.

59

S. Thake

PROCUREMENT AND PRODUCTIVITY – THE SCOPE FOR CHANGE

Industrialisation Forum 1974 *5* (1–2) pp 9–18

It is suggested that although competitive bidding procedures dominate in the public sector it is necessary to change them, in order to benefit from the potential for continuity. Obstacles to efficiency are traced to instability, discontinuity, and the lack of uniform contract conditions. Serial and continuity contracts allow for greater productivity, and industrialisation is highly desirable, in terms of improved and reduced cost of buildings.

58
G. Wigglesworth and D. Wisdom
PROCUREMENT METHODS THEIR EFFECT ON THE INDUSTRIALISATION OF BUILDING
Industrialisation Forum 1974 *5* (1–2) pp 19–28
Organising demand for building through procurement policies is discussed with reference to the public sector houseing, and educational fields. It is concluded that system building did not receive sustained orders to amortize plant costs and consequently contractors returned to traditional methods of house building. The number of closed systems for educational building is felt to have defeated long term objectives, the influence of such systems on the process of industrialisation generally is regarded as small.

57
M. Green
IN PRAISE OF THE PACKAGE DEAL
Construction News 1974 January 24. pp 28
The advantages of the package deal are outlined.

56
Associated General Contractors of America
'CM FOR THE GENERAL CONTRACTOR – A GUIDE MANUAL FOR CONSTRUCTION MANAGEMENT'
1974, pp 161
An examination is made of the differences between construction (project) management (CM) and traditional contractual methods. Sections include an overview of CM; selling CM services and negotiating the contract; planning and scheduling; estimating and budgeting: CM control system; procurement and construction. Appendices provide details of the function of the CN during planning and construction phases; a standard form of contract; and a standard form of sub-contract.

55
CPRE
'DEVELOPMENT CONTROL PACKAGE BUILDINGS'
1974, pp 34
Weaknesses in countryside planning and development controls are identified. It is estimated that some 80% of all agricultural buildings will contain a package element within 20 years. In most cases the design will offer no flexibility, yet planning procedures are concerned with building appearance only after an application has been submitted. Consequently it is considered that controls must be exercised at the blueprint stage before costly manufacturing processes have been set up. It is suggested that a central agency be set up to public criteria and principles for design and to award certification for finishes and cladding.

1973

54
J. Dunaway
MANAGEMENT CONTRACTS – A PSA VIEW
Construction (DOE) 1973 December, pp 29–30
The principles of management contracting and its advantages are discussed.

53
P. W. G. Morris
ORGANISATIONAL ANALYSIS OF PROJECT MANAGEMENT IN THE BUILDING INDUSTRY
Build International 1973 *6* November/December, pp 595–616
The way in which the systems approach can help a project management function and the kinds of forces which shape a particular projects information requirements are studied. Attention is paid to the problems of bridging the design-construction gap and organisation theory is used to examine the pattern of co-ordination and control in the building process.

52
N. Cameron and P. Pearson
PLANNING AND CONTROLLING 'DESIGN AND CONSTRUCT' PROJECTS Building 1973 *224* April 13, pp 115–116, 119–120
The building and equipping of new offices under a package deal contract is described with reference to the design brief and placing the contract, client's management procedure, working procedure, main contractor's role, cost control and project planning.

51
J. Carter
TECHNICAL STUDY. INTEGRATED DESIGN AND CONSTRUCTION: ESSO MOTOR HOTEL AT BRISTOL
Architects Journal 1973 *157* March 21, pp 707–714
Looks at an integrated design and construction project and shows how a package deal provided, arguably a quicker answer than more traditional methods. The project, a 156 bedroom motel, has air-conditioned conference accommodation for 400, a restaurant for 200 and a one-acre (0.4ha) artificial lake. Progress month by month is tabulated at the end of the article.

50
J. Carter
MANAGEMENT CONTRACTING: THE HORIZON PROJECT
Architects Journal 1973 *157* February 14, pp 395–400
The management contracting procedures employed, with Bovis Fee as the management contractor, in the construction of a cigarette factory are described with the events being given in diary form.

49
COMPETITION v NEGOTIATION – MANAGEMENT CONTRACTING
Architectural Design 1973 *43* (3), pp 197

48
MAKING A CONTRACT – THE PACKAGE DEAL
Building Trades Journal 1973 *166* February 16, pp 22, 24, 28.
The package deal contract is examined in the context of larger projects and an outline given of some of the necessary procedures in its negotiation.

47
RICS
THE CHARTERED QUANTITY SURVEYOR AND PACKAGE CONTRACTS"
1973 (Pamphlet)
Disadvantages of package deals are summarised although it is accepted that under certain circumstances the system can be advantageous to the client. It is stated that considerable evidence is available to show that the appointment of a quantity surveyor by the building owner results in substantial financial savings to the owner.

46
MUNTER PROJECT – DRAFT OF DOCUMENTATION FOR EARLY TENDERING
National Swedish Building Research Summary R74: 1973, pp2
It is considered that existing recommendations in Sweden are not adjusted to invitation of tenders and contracting resulting in package deal contracts or early tendering. Draft instructions are outlined for the drawing up of documentation for contracts between client and contractor.

45
J. B. Cannel
PACKAGE DEAL AND THE PROFESSIONS
Chartered Surveyor – Building and Quantity Surveying Quarterly 1973 *1* September, pp 7–9
The package deal concept is evaluated and the conclusion made that there is no evidence of the final cost or contract time under a package deal being very different from those found with traditional methods. Without proper control by the client it is suggested that the cost could be significantly higher.

1972

44
J. Carter
MANAGEMENT CONTRACTING
Architects Journal 1972 *156* December 13, pp 1371–1674
The climate is assessed for the development of management contracting, described as the appointment of the contractor to join the design team to assist in working out the design, programme the work and run the job on site. This is followed by an outline of how the contract is managed and a discussion of the responsibilities carried by the respective members of the team. Finally the advantages to the design team and the contractor are evaluated.

43
J. Anderson
CHARTERED SURVEYORS AND THE PACKAGE DEAL
Chartered Surveyor 1972 *105* October, pp 173–174
A report is given of a survey to establish the types of service and advice given by surveyors to clients when retained to assist and advise on package deal projects. Following an outline of the package deals available and the services offered by the contractors, replies to questions are reported dealing with the problems encountered in relation to the form of contract, difficulties with variations and extras, control exercised by client's surveyor, defects liability period, methods of payment, and fee scale.

42
E. V. Broadbent
TRENDS IN CONSTRUCTION MANAGEMENT
Building Services Engineer 1972 *40* June, pp 75–78
The problems are discussed which arise from the traditional separation of development, design and construction and in particular of the harmful effects of divided responsibility. The benefits of package dealing in mitigating some of these problems are presented.

41
J. Chisholm
AGAINST THE PACKAGE DEAL
Architect 1972 May, pp 49–50
The main criticism of the package deal is that it contributes to a further lowering of architectural standards which are unlikely to improve when the main criteria for new building is pre-determined cost and speed of erection.

40
W. J. Shergold
COMPUTER AIDS IN CONTRACT LETTING AND CONTROL FOR CIVIL ENGINEERING AND BUILDING CONTRACTS
Paper Seminar on Tendering Procedures, April 1972, pp 20.
Following an outline of the types of contract available, e.g. package deal, lump sum, and measurement, the provision of a schedule of rates is discussed in relation to its computerisation.

39
J. A. Summers
UNITED KINGDOM/FRENCH TENDERING PROCEDURES
Paper RICS 'Anglo-French Collaboration in Property Development and Management' Conference, Paris, April 1972, pp 4 (in English and French).
An outline of UK tendering procedures only is given.

38
CONSTRUCTION MANAGEMENT: PUTTING PROFESSIONALISM INTO CONTRACTING
Construction Methods and Equipment 1972 *54* March, pp 59–75
Guidelines are presented for practising construction management which comprises project planning, design and construction as integrated tasks within a construction system consisting of the client, construction manager and architect/engineer. The team works from project inception to completion, interactions between cost, quality and completion schedule being carefully examined so that a project of maximum value to the client is realised in the most economic time scale. Directly related to US practice some personal views of the advantages obtained are presented.

37
N. P. Golds
CURRENT CONTRACTING METHODS
Construction (DoE), 1972 (1) March, pp 23–37
Following a brief outline of the historical development of the current contractual arrangements, the various forms of tender and contract at present in use are examined.

36
A. E. Thomas
'MANAGEMENT CONTRACTING'
IOB Site Management Information Service Paper No. 46,
1972, pp 6
The benefits of management contracting are discussed
which as a result of involving the management team at
the design stage can lead to greater site efficiency and
improve the client's chances of gaining from a competitive
situation, since all works are quoted for, including those
normally included under the main contractor's services.
The concept is highly flexible and there is virtually no type
of scheme on which it would be anything but beneficial.
A lower limit of £250,000 may be necessary to ensure
economic viability.

35
W. B. Foxhall
**'PROFESSIONAL CONSTRUCTION MANAGEMENT
AND PROJECT ADMINISTRATION'**
1972, AIA and Architectural Record, pp 114
Professional construction management is seen as the co-
ordination of the skills that allows the project to run
orderly and with the greatest efficiency: it must be a
professional service since it participates in a role of agency
toward the client rather than drawing on the profit margin
in a construction contract. The component skills and functions are identified and related to the central professional
requirements of time, cost and quality control.

34
Architects in Industry Group
**'THE ARCHITECT AND THE PACKAGE DEAL – A
CASE FOR PROPER RECOGNITION'**
1972, pp 4
This report considers the concept of package deals, its
advantages and limitations, and the role of the architect
and quantity surveyor. It recommends that the RIBA
should give greater recognition to the package deal as a
legitimate form of practice for its members; that the JCT
should produce a form of practice appropriate to the particular requirements of the package deal; and that notes
for guidance be produced for those intending to operate
within or use the package deal system showing the rights
and obligations of the participants and the advantages and
limitations of this type of contract.

33
J. Lundeberg
**ARCHITECTS AND PROBLEMS – A STUDY OF THE
INITIAL STAGE OF A PACKAGE DEAL CONTRACT**
National Swedish Building Research Summary R37:
1972, pp 2
This study, based on tape recorded material of four
meetings, covers observation and analysis of the sequence
of events and solutions found to problems during the
initial stage of work on the tender document. One
interesting facet is the conflict between the architects
and contractors systems of assessing a situation.

32
**CONSTRUCTION MANAGEMENT. PART 2 – THE
MAN BEHIND THE CONCEPT**
Construction Methods and Equipment 1972 *54* April,
pp 110–118
The attitude of individuals in the US construction industry to the concept of management contracting and in
particular the general contractor's viewpoint are expressed. The application of management contracting
to three projects is considered and the results of each
operation examined.

31
Associated General Contractors of America
'CONSTRUCTION MANAGEMENT GUIDELINES'
1972, pp 10
A simple guide is given to construction (project) management (CM), the formation of the CM team, selection
and functions.

1971

30
D. R. Harper
**EVALUATION OF ALTERNATIVE METHODS OF
CONTRACTOR SELECTION**
Paper to UMIST Conference at International Building
Exhibition, London, November 1971, pp 2
The developments which have made competitive
tendering less and less attractive and led to the
introduction of other forms of contractor selection are
summarised.

29
R. Jones
**GROWTH AND DEVELOPMENT OF PACKAGE
DEALS**
Building Trades Journal 1971 *163* July 30, pp 12–13
It is suggested that from the contractor's viewpoint he
will take the best from the professional side and
match it with his own abilities in the management,
co-ordination and economic fields. The components
of the package deal are described and the benefits
to the client outlined. Marketing of the service is also
discussed.

28
J. Weller
PACKAGING THE FACTORY FARM
RIBA Journal 1971 *78* May, pp 194–199
The reasons are discussed for the firm entrenchment of
the package deal in farm building. It is considered that
the central role of package deal building in agriculture
reflects a revolution which must take place in other
spheres of specialised design and construction, and
is bound to have profound implications for architects.

27
R. Jones
**GROWTH AND DEVELOPMENT OF PACKAGE
DEALS**
Paper, Institute of Marketing, Construction Industry
Market Group Meeting, May 1971, pp 11
The various parts comprising the package deal
concept and the marketing of this service are
described. In the ensuing discussion the place of
the architect was considered and differing views
were expressed regarding whether the architect
should be employed within the contractor's organisation.

26
NEGOTIATED HOUSING – WHATS IN STORE FOR THE PACKAGE DEAL?
Surveyor 1971 March 12, pp 28–29
The current situation in the public sector where the negotiated contract has virtually disappeared is discussed in relation to the deleterious effect that it is having on system builders.

25
G. Ericson
VALUATION OF TENDERS AT PACKAGE DEAL CONTRACTS
National Swedish Building Research Summary R24: 1971, pp 2
A system is described to enable the client to make a choice from a number of tenders. Applied to a project for one-family houses it was found that in this case mathematical evaluation systems of this type do not give unambiguous results due to uncertainty of weighting and marketing when differences between the tenders are small.

24
Association of Professional Engineers of the Province of Ontario
'PERFORMANCE STANDARDS FOR PROJECT MANAGEMENT AND SCALE OF FEES FOR PROJECT MANAGEMENT SERVICES'
1971, pp 11
The standards of performance to be expected for the management of planning, design, construction, and commissioning of a capital project within a cost budget and prescribed time schedule are described.

1970

23
J. Carter
PACKAGE DEALS 3: CLIENTS AND CONCLUSIONS
Architects Journal 1970 *152* November 25, pp 1263–1265
Comments on their reasons for choosing a package deal are given by a number of clients who have had industrial buildings constructed. Although the selection of a package dealer was based on varying factors it did appear that dealing with the one organisation was significant; of particular importance was the impression that there was a lack of specialisation among architects in this field in contrast to an increasing number of package dealers. In conclusion it is considered that the private architectural practice as a building management organisation is no longer economically viable and nor is it able to provide a specialist service for an increasing demand. This implies that the contractor will become increasingly the clients first contact and leader of the building team, perhaps leading to the architect becoming a 'space and planner-subcontractor'. To retain his position there needs to be a repeal of the directorship ban altogether with a revaluation of the architects education to remedy the urgent and essential need for a common understanding between architects and builders. As an immediate measure the setting up by architects of contracting organisations is proposed with the RIBA providing an advisory service for members.

22
J. Carter
PACKAGE DEALS 2 PORTRAITS OF FIVE FIRMS
Architects Journal 1970 *152* November 18, pp 1203–1207
General details are given relating to the structure and operation of four unnamed package dealers and The Building Design Partnership.

21
J. Carter
PACKAGE DEALS 1: WHY PACKAGE DEALS?
Architects Journal 1970 *152* November 11, pp 1155–1156
Indications are that package dealing has increased considerably in the last few years and results of a limited survey show that one sixth of larger contractors provide an all-in service to the extent of 20% or more of their turnover. The origins of the package deal are outlined and the reason for their present development considered in relation to the concept of the architect as an artist and as the client's adviser.

20
PROGRAMMED TENDERING FOR ALBERTA UNIVERSITY BUILDING
Building 1970 *219* August 21, pp 64
Under the procedure briefly outlined the contractor acts in a project management capacity calling and awarding contracts in consultation with the university. The procedure is expected to allow construction to begin 4-6 months earlier than normal.

19
REAL PACKAGE DEAL
Architects Journal 1970 *152* July 22, pp 169 (Editorial)
A new package deal service developed by E. E. Chivers m Sons does not simply combine design and building but is a true package deal. They find alternative means of financing the project and a choice of sites, and this is followed by recommending an architect and if necessary a quantity surveyor. It is considered that this sophisticated form of package deal is the real threat to the future of the architects' practice.

18
Lord Mais
ROLE OF THE QUANTITY SURVEYOR. THERE ARE NOT ENOUGH PRACTICAL PEOPLE
Illustrated Carpenter & Builder 1970 *161* July 17, pp 17–20
An interview ranging over topics such as the amalgamation of the IQS and RICS, technician training, the future role of the quantity surveyor, and the effect of the package deal on the quantity surveyor in private practice.

17
O. Luder
OTHER SIDE OF THE PACKAGE DEAL
Construction Steelwork 1970 June, pp 6, 8, 10
The reasons for the increase in package dealing are outlined. It is considered that the client loses two valuable advantages by deciding upon a package deal; the independent advice of the architect and the ability to obtain competitive tenders for the work. A suitable alternative put forward is to employ the services of an integrated design consortium and the contractor selected by negotiation or open tendering. Although mainly concerned with illustrating the potential disadvantages of the

package deal the author accepts that it has its merits but makes a plea that the client consider every alternative before deciding by which method he should obtain his new building.

16
A. Wates
PACKAGE DEAL BY ANY OTHER NAME THAN WATES
Building Design 1970 June 26, pp 6–7
An interview regarding Wates' contractor consultancy system which involves the contractor in bringing together a management and specialist team to provide a service to the developer or architect.

15
R. B. Hellard
TWO STAGE PACKAGE DEALS
Architects Journal 1970 *151* April 1, pp 792–793
The new procedure proposed involves the design team forming part of a new multi disciplinary management unit – 'the project management group' – which would, through its design team, prepare and design, obtain tenders from selected contractors, and then put in a comprehensive tender for the whole project. The client would be free to accept the tender or to reject it, pay the design fees only, and seek alternative tenders for building the group's design.

14
R. G. Orr
CASE FOR THE PACKAGE DEAL
Construction Steelwork and Metals 1970 March, pp 24, 26–27
The main arguments for the package deal are discussed, with particular reference to marketing, specialisation, responsibility, costs and price, and collaboration with consultants.

13
E. D. Jefferies Matthews
IF WE MUST HAVE PACKAGE DEALS . . .
Construction News 1970, March 19, pp 10
It is considered that to fully safeguard the clients interest it is desirable for an architect to provide a brief in a form which enables the contractor to obtain a complete picture of the requirements and give him a sound basis for his estimates.

12
J. R. Lowe
THE CONSULTANT'S CASE AGAINST PACKAGE DEALS
Construction News 1970 January 8, pp 18
Examples are presented to illustrate the danger to the client of a package deal. It is shown that the client can obtain an inferior or unsuitable product and not necessarily in a shorter time. Although it is accepted that there is a place for package deals it is maintained that the use of a professional team will provide a better and cheaper design.

11
P. Janson
PACKAGE DEALS
National Swedish Building Research Summary R47: 1970, pp 2
This study shows that with the package deal the client has little scope for controlling design rationally and consequently there should be some compensation. Although lower prices are claimed by package dealing there is a danger that monopolies will be formed with the result that prices will increase.

10
Ministry of Public Buildings & Works
'THE BUILDING PROCESS: A CASE STUDY FROM MARKS & SPENCER LTD'.
1970, HMSO. pp 60
The way is described in which a large commercial organisation meets its continuous need for new buildings or extensions to existing ones. The study is in six parts covering background information, the building programme, the building process – design and site operations, computer preparation and pricing of bills of quantities, and evaluation of the performance of the organisation. Appendices give examples of monthly cost statement, budgetary data, form of contract between the company and its main contractor, minutes of typical meetings, priced locational bills, item location and materials and labour scheduling.

9
General Services Administration – Public Buildings Service
'CONSTRUCTION CONTRACTING SYSTEMS – A REPORT ON THE SYSTEMS USED BY PBS AND OTHER ORGANISATIONS'
1970, pp 150 **4** appendices
An evaluation is made, in relation to experience gained by the American Public Building Service, of the conventional firm price lump sum contract and why in the interests of efficiency and productivity other forms of letting a contract needed to be examined. It is concluded that turnkey contracts can provide significant benefits on simple design projects and that management contracting is suitable for large and/or complex projects.

1969

8
R. G. Orr
CASE FOR THE PACKAGE DEAL
Construction News 1969 December 4, pp 22–23

7
CLIENT EDUCATION IS KEY TO PACKAGE DEAL SUCCESS
Construction News 1969 *89* July 10, pp 10

6
C. J. Platten
PACKAGE DEAL IN PERSPECTIVE
Architect and Building News 1969 March 13, pp 36–39

5
L. W. Madden
PACKAGE DEALING
Building 1969 *216* February 21, pp 147–148, 150
Studies have shown that the procedure is on the increase
and for this reason it would be helpful to everybody if
more design-and-build examples were exposed to public
view. Aspects considered in particular are the place of
outside consultants, work handled by architects, house
design-build by contractors, hospitals design and build,
LA's use of design-build and contractor's views on future.

4
O. Luder
PRIVATE ARCHITECT AND THE DEAL
Building 1969 *216* February 7, pp 87–88
Reasons behind the growth of the package deal are summarised. It is believed that the private architect can offer
better service than the package dealer but only if he is
willing to make some radical changes in the method of
practice.

1968

3
R. Bidgood
ARCHITECTS AND PACKAGE DEALS
System Building and Design 1968 October, pp 63–66;
1969 January, pp 43–46. 1969 May, pp 51–54
The architect's involvement in various types of package
deal are described and the methods of organisation and
implementation are discussed, together with the reasons
why a professional practice could be packaged. The two
main types of package deal are considered and the advantages to be participants indicated.

2
J. Gwynn
PACKAGE DEAL THREAT
Consulting Engineer 1968 *32* July, pp 59–64

1967

1
H. Hicks
MANAGEMENT AND THE PACKAGE DEAL
Proceedings 10B Annual Conference, Harrogate 1967,
pp 9–12
The philosophy of a package deal contractor is outlined
and details provided of his method of operation. Advan-
tages to the client and his safeguards are considered.